THE
SHROPSI
WAY

A comprehensive guide to the recently extended and
upgraded long distance walking route exploring
the stunning varied scenery and fascinating history of
the beautiful county of Shropshire.
It offers various multi-day walks and 33 linear walks
linked to public transport,
with detailed route descriptions, maps,
historical content and practical information.

David Berry

KITTIWAKE

About the author

David is an experienced walker with an interest in local history. He is the author of a series of Kittiwake walks guidebooks covering North Wales where he has lived and worked for many years. He has been a freelance writer for Walking Wales magazine, worked as a Rights of Way surveyor across North Wales and served as a member of Denbighshire Local Access Forum.

Whether on a riverside ramble or mountain walk he greatly appreciates the beauty, culture and history of the landscape and hopes that his comprehensive guidebooks will encourage people to explore on foot its diverse scenery and rich heritage. He has undertaken many long distance walks, including coast-to-coast crossings of England, Scotland and Wales, and created three long distance routes of his own: The Dee Way, The Conwy Valley Way and The Mawddach-Ardudwy Trail.
For more information visit: www.davidberrywalks.co.uk

Acknowledgments
I wish to thank Jim Stabler, Shropshire Council's Access Development Officer for the Shropshire Way, now retired, Andrew Lipa, RoW officer and staff in the Shropshire Archives in Shrewsbury for their assistance. Also to Ian and Betina at Severn House Campsite, Montford Bridge for their hospitality during my stays there. Finally to the many interesting and helpful people I met upon the way.

Published by Kittiwake Books Limited
3 Glantwymyn Village Workshops, Glantwymyn, Machynlleth, Montgomeryshire SY20 8LY

Printed by Mixam, UK.

ISBN: 978 1 908748 31 7

Contents

INTRODUCTION

The Shropshire Way

The Shropshire Way long distance walk explores the beautiful historic border county of Shropshire. It was originally created by local Rambler Association groups and Shropshire walking clubs in consultation with Shropshire County Council and completed in 1980. The main section was a loop between Wem and Ludlow, with a western branch from Bridges over Stiperstones to Bishop's Castle and Clun to rejoin the main route on Hopesay Hill. There was also a short branch north from Wem past Whitchurch to Grindley Brook, where it linked with the Sandstone Trail.

In 2007 Shropshire County Council set out to relaunch the Shropshire Way. Following wide consultation with individual or groups of local walkers, who suggested route deviations or alternative footpaths, work began to improve the original route and extend the trail further across the county. The project was steered by a Liaison Group and led by a Project Officer, in partnership with Shropshire Ramblers, walking and volunteer groups, landowners and individuals.

In 2008 the southern section around the Shropshire Hills was extensively upgraded and newly waymarked. Minor route alterations were made to take in places of interest and viewpoints. New links were created from Wilderhope Manor on Wenlock Edge to Craven Arms and via Church Stretton to the Long Mynd. Another went from Titterstone Clee Hill to Cleobury Mortimer and on to join the Severn Way.

Work then continued on the planned second phase to extend the trail around parts of less well known North Shropshire, linking places of scenic or historical interest through the creation of new route sections, upgraded and waymarked in stages. A third phase, already mapped out, covers Shrewsbury and the central area, with links to Wellington. The Shropshire Way currently consists of 27 linked route sections, covering a total of 297 miles, almost doubling the length of the original trail. I understand that eventually further new links to Market Drayton and Bridgnorth will be created.

The Shropshire Way now offers a comprehensive network of route sections that can be tailored to individual requirements, providing opportunities for multi-day walks of varying length, as well as linear day walks linked to public transport. At its heart is Shrewsbury, whose mainline station on the

National Rail Network, facilitates easy access from and to anywhere in Britain. The Shropshire Way is promoted and maintained by Shropshire Council, with a comprehensive web-site and two booklets, with a third planned.

As a walks guidebook writer in North Wales I seek my recreational walking pleasure from undertaking long distance trails in other parts of Britain. I had wanted to do the Shropshire Way for a long time and in the late autumn of 2013 I finally spent several days walking the western Shropshire Hills section. It was a memorable short trip with stunning scenery and full of interest. On my return I contacted the Shropshire Council officer responsible for developing the Shropshire Way to provide positive feedback as well as details of broken stiles etc that I had noted on the way.

Arising from that conversation came the idea of a Kittiwake guidebook. The revised Shropshire Way, while opening up more of the beautiful countryside for walkers, is now more complex in nature, with multiple choices. I felt that there was a need to bring the complete network of routes into one guidebook, with guidance on how best to use it to explore Shropshire's diverse scenery and rich heritage. It would complement the existing material, providing for the first time detailed route descriptions and more historical content. I decided to walk the Shropshire Way in a clockwise direction and approached it from the initial perspective of a long distance walker, whilst researching its potential for linear day walks linked to public transport.

Walking the route sections was quite a logistical challenge. Using a combination of car, buses and trains, either from a campsite base near Shrewsbury, or on long trips from home, I walked most of the trail as day walks. The remainder was completed as a continuous backpacking walk. Afterwards I provided the Council with written feedback on the trail, highlighting specific issues I had encountered. Interpreting the trail for a guidebook then presented its own challenges, but I hope that you find it both helpful and informative as you explore on foot this wonderful county.

The guidebook offers:

– detailed route descriptions with accompanying maps, historical content, guidance and practical information to help people walk the Shropshire Way.

– a continuous variable long distance circular trail of up to 202 ¼ miles around Shropshire.

– a continuous variable long distance circular trail of up to 98½ miles around North Shropshire and up to 119¼ miles around South Shropshire.

– other suggested shorter multi-day walks.

– 33 linear day walks linked to public transport covering most route sections.

– routes that incorporate diverse scenic landscape features, stunning viewpoints, historic towns and villages, ancient highways, Iron Age hillforts, castles, and other sites of historical interest.

– a fascinating insight into the history of Shropshire and the various communities that the trail passes through.

Shropshire

Shropshire is one of the largest and most rural counties in England, adjoining the border with Wales, and renowned for its varied beautiful landscape. Previously known as Salop, the county, with Shrewsbury at its heart, forms two distinctive halves, reflecting its diverse geology and character. North Shropshire is largely a flat fertile plain extending west to a more rugged upland border edge. It has its own small lakeland of glacial meres near Ellesmere and the third largest lowland raised peat bog in Britain, now a National Nature Reserve. By contrast South Shropshire features a range of hills, woods and river valleys. A quarter of its area forms the Shropshire Hills Area of Outstanding Natural Beauty, designated in 1958. The hills vary greatly in character. The Long Mynd with its long moorland plateau and steep side valleys contrasts with the distinctive craggy top of nearby Stiperstones. The Clee hills are shaped by mining and quarrying, whilst the Wrekin dominates the county's eastern landscape. In between is Wenlock Edge, a major wooded limestone escarpment. These are well known Shropshire hills, but there are other rolling hills of great beauty to discover. The upland pasture and heathland, combine with the attractive river valleys, ancient woodland and long established field systems to provide a wonderful habitat for a wide range of wildlife. There are numerous nature reserves across the county, 40 of them managed by the Shropshire Wildlife Trust.

However it is not just Shropshire's beautiful varied countryside that makes the county so attractive. It has a rich heritage that reveals man's impact on the landscape over many centuries. There are Iron Age hillforts and Bronze Age burial sites, ancient field systems and many medieval settlements, ancient trackways, and Roman roads. There are relics of the county's important industrial past, when areas were mined and quarried for coal, lead, copper, zinc, iron ore, sandstone, limestone and dhutstone. Most notably the

Ironbridge Gorge – a centre of the Industrial Revolution, and now a World Heritage site. Crossing the northern part of the county are the Montgomery and Llangollen canals – part of an early national transport network, which once also included the now disused Shrewsbury Canal. During the 19th C the arrival of the railway brought a new era of more efficient transport throughout Shropshire, but the county now carries the legacy of many branch lines closed in the 1960s.

One man in particular has left his mark on the county's landscape – Thomas Telford (1757-1834), the famous Scottish civil engineer, stonemason and architect, who was at one time the Surveyor of Public Works for Shropshire. His pioneering engineering legacy in the county is immense: canals, aqueducts, road bridges, and the London-Holyhead coach road. He was also involved in the renovation of Shrewsbury Castle and prison, as well as churches. The new town of Telford in east Shropshire, now part of a separate unitary authority, was named in his honour in 1968.

The border with Wales has for centuries posed a particular challenge for England's rulers and played a significant role in Shropshire's history. As the Anglo Saxon kingdom of Mercia extended further westwards into the Welsh kingdom of Powys, the border was defined during the 8thC by the building of Wat's Dyke then the more substantial Offa's Dyke earthwork. Later, after William the Conqueror's invasion in 1066, he granted large areas of land along the border to his loyal Norman barons, as a strategic defence against the Welsh. They became Marcher Lords overseeing the border territories, with the right to administer laws and run their estates, virtually independent of the monarchy. The county was the central part of the Welsh Marches, which is still known as the Marches today. They built castles across the county and established important market towns such as Shrewsbury, Ludlow, Clun, Bishop's Castle and Oswestry. These towns and others complement the county's many attractive ancient villages with sandstone churches, timber-framed houses and country pubs.

For centuries changing agricultural practices have helped shape Shropshire's varied landscape. About 86% of the land is devoted to agriculture, making the county one of the UK's most important sources of food production. Agriculture plays an important part in the county's economy and landscape management.Over a third of agricultural land is used for arable crops, mainly barley, wheat, potatoes, and sugar beet. Other land is used by livestock, mainly sheep, dairy and beef cattle, or for hay/silage-making.

Shrewsbury

The county town of Shrewsbury, lying within a loop of the beautiful river Severn, is one of the most stunning medieval towns in England, with a rich heritage. It is said that the area may have first attracted people from the former Roman fort of Viroconium (Wroxeter), Britains fourth largest Roman settlement, a few miles to the south east. Its name originates from the Anglo-Saxon settlement of 'Scrobbesbyrig' (fortified place in scrubland) established near fords across the loop of the river. It was first recorded in 901 as an important fortified border settlement within the kingdom of Mercia. After the Norman Conquest, Roger de Montgomery was created Earl of Shrewsbury and he founded a substantial castle here in1074, to complement the river defence, and an abbey as a Benedictine Monastery in 1083 on the site of a Saxon church. By the mid 13thC a fortified walled market town linked to the castle had been built and a thriving trade in leather and wool established. It was then one of the largest towns in England.

However, during the 13thC the town was subjected to regular Welsh attacks, until Dafydd ap Gruffydd, the last Prince of Wales, was defeated by Edward I in 1283. Parliament was summoned to Shrewsbury to decide Dafydd's fate and he was subsequently hung, drawn and quartered in the town. The castle was strengthened and a period of peace followed. In 1403, just north of the town there occurred one of the bloodiest battles in English history. In a few hours thousands were killed in Henry IV's victory over rebel forces led by Harry Percy (Hotspur).

In 1540 the Abbey fell victim to Henry VIII's Dissolution of the Monasteries, but part continued to be used to the present day as a Parish church. In 1552 Edward VI founded Shrewsbury School, which quickly became one of England's largest and is held in high regard to the present day. One of its earlier buildings opposite the castle is now the town library. During the English Civil War Shrewsbury was a Royalist stronghold, but fell to Parliamentary forces in 1645. After 1663 the castle became privately owned until 1924, then restored and now houses the Shropshire Regimental Museum.

During the 16thC wool became the major trade, with the town serving as the finishing centre of Welsh cloth. The river became its primary trade route and quays and warehouses adorned the riverbank near the Welsh Bridge. The town prospered and many fine buildings were erected. By the 18thC it was an important staging post on the London-Holyhead coach route to Ireland. By the century end it had its own canal, later linked to the national canal network.

The town remained largely unchanged by the industrial revolution, despite the prominence of Ironbridge. However it can lay claim to the origin of modern day skyscrapers, for in the suburb of Ditherington, is a five storey flax mill built in 1797, which is the oldest iron-framed building in the world. During the 19thC Shrewsbury became an important railway town, the hub of a network of lines through the county. Shrewsbury's most famous son was Charles Darwin, the naturalist and scientist whose theory of evolution changed our knowledge of life on Earth. He was born in the town in 1809 and educated at Shrewsbury School.

Nowadays Shrewsbury, pronounced in two different ways: 'Shrows-bury' or 'Shroos-bury', with a population of about 100,000, is a thriving unspoilt market town, with many attractions for visitors. It offers a wide range of independent shops, cafes, restaurants, and traditional pubs. The town is famous for its annual Flower Show and also hosts one of the country's top folk festivals. It has a network of medieval streets and alleyways, with over 660 listed buildings. At its heart lies The Square, the centre of the town's economic and cultural life for centuries, as well as an important meeting place. It contains one of the town's finest buildings – the Old Market Hall built in 1596 to replace a previous 13thC market building. The two-storey building reflected Shrewsbury prosperity as a regional trading centre. Cloth was sold in the upper room and corn on the lower floor. From 1870 – 1995 it was used as the county magistrates court, and currently houses a popular film theatre and café bar. It is the ideal place to start and finish the Shropshire Way.

Overview of the Shropshire Way

The trail conveniently falls into two separate areas of the county. I have described each route section to facilitate clockwise circuits of both North and South Shropshire, starting and finishing at Shrewsbury.

North Shropshire (sections 1–23)

The northern part of the Shropshire Way is generally pastoral and peaceful in nature. Whilst predominantly mixed farmland, it is full of interest. It features old market towns, attractive ancient villages with red sandstone churches and traditional country pubs, scenic canals, meres and mosses, nature reserves, country park sites, and the fascinating Lime Works Heritage site at

Llanymynech. Its western upland border section offers delightful woodland, old Oswestry racecourse and impressive sections of the 8thC Offa's Dyke earthwork.

After a section of delightful riverside walking in Shrewsbury the Shropshire Way heads to Montford Bridge, then continues past ancient churches and a little known castle site to Nesscliffe. After passing through Nesscliffe Countryside Heritage Site, with its Iron Age fort and legendary cave it continues to Kinton and the early 15thC church in Melverley, It then follows the River Vyrnwy as it meanders through farmland to reach the small border community of Llanymynech. Here one route heads along the Montgomery Canal, while the main route intermittently follows the Offa's Dyke Path, across the part wooded undulating borderland, past a link to Oswestry, through historic Oswestry Racecourse, and over Selattyn Hill. The trail then heads east along the Ceiriog valley to Chirk Bank, close to the Welsh border town of Chirk.

The next section to the small attractive town of Ellesmere is mainly along the popular Llangollen Canal, being joined by the other canal route from Llanymynech at Lower Frankton junction. The route continues along the canal past other meres, then diverts to visit two parts of Fenn's, Whixall and Bettisfield Mosses National Nature Reserve. It then heads to a junction of branches near the border hamlet of Welsh End. The main branch continues south across farmland via Edstaston village, with its gem of a church, to the small town of Wem. The other makes a long circuitous link via two interesting nature reserves to the attractive market town of Whitchurch, then extends to Grindley Brook. However, in order to include Whitchurch and enjoy its link section, it is better to continue along the Llangollen Canal to the junction with the Whitchurch Branch, then follow the Shropshire Way route into Whitchurch.

From Wem there are two Shropshire Way branches, which formed part of the original main circular route. One heads south through farmland, featuring the ancient communities of Grinshall, famous for its sandstone, Hadnall and Astley to Haughmond Abbey, before heading west to Shrewsbury. The other heads more or less south east through the attractive ancient villages of Lee Brockhurst, Stanton upon Hine Heath and High Ercall to Isombridge Farm, then continues to the market town of Wellington.

South Shropshire (sections 24–61)

The southern part of the Shropshire Way takes you through Shropshire Hills AONB and adjoining attractive countryside, visiting various historic market towns and places of interest. It is more undulating and demanding in nature, but the effort required to cross the county's highest hills is rewarded by stunning scenery and breathtaking views.

The Shropshire Way leaves Shrewsbury and heads east to Haugmond Abbey, passes through popular Houghmond Hill woodland site, then continues across farmland to the attractive village of Wrockwardine and the market town of Wellington. The next section starts with a climb through ancient woodland, then onto The Wrekin, probably Shropshire's best known hill, with its Iron Age hillfort and finishes with a descent into Ironbridge Gorge, a powerhouse of the industrial revolution and now a World Heritage Site. The trail continues via attractive Benthall Edge Wood to Much Wenlock, the birthplace of the modern Olympic Games, then continues along the famous wooded Wenlock Edge to 16th C Wilderhope Manor, now a youth hostel.

From here you can now continue along Wenlock Edge, then follow new links to Craven Arms or Church Stretton. However the main original route heads southwards towards the Clee Hills, once extensively mined and quarried. A new loop now takes in the summit of Adon Burf, Shropshire's highest hill (1771 ft/540 metres). It then visits Brown Clee Hill's second peak of Clee Burf and continues south across Titterstone Clee hill. A new link heads east to Cleobury Mortimer and on to join the Severn Way. The main route continues to Angel Bank then heads westwards across farmland to the low-lying Iron Age hillfort of Caynham Camp and to the historic fortified town of Ludlow, with its splendid castle and reputation for fine food. This is the most southerly point of the Shropshire Way.

The trail now heads along the edge of the Teme valley to the attractive hamlet of Bromfield, then continues to stunning medieval Stokesay Castle and the Discovery Centre at the small railway town of Craven Arms. Here there are a choice of routes to Church Stretton. One follows new links onto Wenlock Edge and north to Ragleth Hill, offering extensive views, overlooking the town. From here new links take you up Carding Mill Valley onto the Long Mynd and along the Port Way, an ancient upland trackway, to join the link from Bridges for the onward walk to Shrewsbury. Another follows the main route from Craven Arms west up to Hopesay Hill, then northwards down to the Onny valley on a long steady climb to Black Knoll (1361 ft/415 metres), before an enjoyable leg stretch on the Port Way, along the broad Long Mynd ridge, to join the link path down to Church Stretton, or an alternative one to Bridges.

From Craven Arms a longer undulating recommended route takes you through a beautiful timeless 'back of beyond' part of the borderlands and Shropshire Hills AONB, featuring two historic relatively remote Norman

Ludlow Castle

border towns. It first follows an undulating route westwards to Hopesay Hill and down to secluded Hopesay village. It later crosses impressive Bury Ditches Iron Age hillfort to reach Clun, Shropshire's smallest town, with its ruined castle. The undulating trail continues northwestwards, crossing the Cefns, a delightful open ridge and Hergan hill to join a section of Offa's Dyke Path. It then heads eastwards to Bishop's Castle. The trail heads to the attractive hamlet of More, then rises onto Linley Hill. Later it continues along the Stiperstones ridge, its National Nature Reserve famous for quartzite outcrops, boasting the second highest point (1759 ft/536 metres) in Shropshire.

From Stiperstones there is a choice of routes to the hamlet of Exford's Green for the link to Shrewsbury, dependent upon accommodation. One route descends to Bridges, with its pub and youth hostel, then goes along a side valley up to join the connecting link along the Port Way from Church Stretton. From here the main route heads northwards, crosses Wilderley Hill, then makes a long steady descent across farmland to Exford's Green. The alternative route is more varied in nature. It continues along the northern end of the Stiperstones ridge, passes through areas of woodland, one containing remains of the area's important lead-mining past. Later it passes around the lower wooded slopes of Earl's Hill Nature Reserve and Pontesford Hill, before continuing across countryside to Longdon village and on to Exford's Green.

The final approach to Shrewsbury crosses Lyth Hill, now a Country Park., which despite its lack of height offers panoramic views. Later it passes through Bayston Hill to reach Rea Brook, from where there is a choice of routes into the heart of Shrewsbury.

Whether on a day walk or multi-day walk I hope you enjoy exploring this beautiful and fascinating border county

SHREWSBURY TO NESSCLIFFE
13 miles

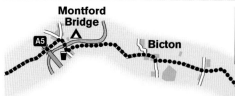

I The Square, Shrewsbury to Montford Bridge
7 miles

Starting from the centre of Shrewsbury the Shropshire Way soon follows a delightful section of the river Severn from the English to the Welsh Bridge. It accompanies the river through Frankwell, quickly leaving the town behind, then continues with it to Shelton. It then follows bridleways through woodland and across farmland to Montford Bridge. The Shropshire Way, which has recently been upgraded, shares this section with the waymarked Severn Way.

From Clive's statue in The Square turn right past Starbucks and continue along the one-way High Street, then along and down Wyle Cop past the Lion Hotel – *a famous coaching inn on the London-Holyhead route, dating from the early 17thC.* Cross another road and continue to English Bridge. *It was built in 1768-74 on the site of an earlier Norman bridge, which had a gate tower and houses. It was rebuilt and widened in 1925.* Take a surfaced path down past houses to walk beside the river,

shortly passing under Greyfriars iron footbridge (1880). Continue along the wide mature tree-lined promenade to the privately-owned Kingsland Toll bridge (1882) – *known locally as the Penny Bridge from the original toll for pedestrians.* Here you have a

choice of riverside routes. (Please note that route a is closed during occasional public events such as the Shrewsbury Flower Show in August.)

For **route a** continue with the riverside promenade along the edge of Quarry Park – *created in 1719 and containing the Dingle, a beautiful sunken garden. The renowned TV gardener, Percy Thrower (1913-88) was its Parks Superintendent* – then cross the elegant Port Hill suspension bridge (1922) to the opposite side.

For **route b** turn right and go up steps onto the bridge. Follow the pavement opposite across the bridge, then descend steps to the riverbank. Follow a riverside path past Shrewsbury School boathouse and Pengwern boat club – *involved* in competitive rowing since the 1870s – then an access road up to the end of Port Hill suspension bridge to join route a.

At the road turn right along the pavement past The Boathouse. Soon turn right on the signposted Severn Way down Water Lane then continue along the riverside promenade to pass under the Welsh Bridge. *This was built in 1793-5 to replace the 12thC St George's bridge. By the 17thC this area was the town's commercial centre, with a thriving river trade.*

2 From beneath Theatre Severn you pass the first of several information boards on a section of Shrewsbury between Frankwell and The Mount – *where Charles Darwin was born in 1809.* The riverside path passes under the Frankwell footbridge (1979), goes along the edge of a car park, then the cricket ground, before bending north into Poplar Island Countryside Site. Continue along the riverside path, passing the West Midland Showground opposite. After a kissing gate follow the narrow enclosed path, then turn left up steps and right before the top to continue with the path above the river. At a road descend steps and continue along the riverside path, passing through Doctor's Field Countryside Site. Continue with the gated riverside path, over a footbridge, and through three fields. The path then rises through trees and continues to Shelton Lane. Go ahead along the road down to the entrance to Mountwood Park, then follow a bridleway through trees. Shortly it descends, continues through the edge of woodland, then rises

steadily. After passing a concrete track on the right, it follows a stony track up to the B4380.

3 Turn right along the roadside path then go along a signposted wide gated bridleway, shortly passing through trees, then going along a field edge onto a stony track. Briefly go along it, then follow the waymarked gated bridleway on the left beside a fence, along the edge of two fields, across another, passing to the right of a pool, then along the next field edge to a road by Rossall Lodge. Go along the driveway opposite to Grove Farm and other properties. Go through a waymarked gate and along a small narrowing field edge to a gate. Follow the bridleway down to another gate, then go half-left up the field and on beside the hedge/tree boundary to a road at Bicton. Go ahead along the road and on the bend continue with the bridleway along the green track ahead, shortly enclosed and bending right, becoming rough in nature. When it splits keep ahead and follow the tree-lined bridleway to a gate. Bear left along a green track towards Montford Bridge, soon descending the field after the track fades and continuing to a bridle gate in the tree boundary ahead. Go slightly right across the next field corner to a partly hidden large footbridge and bridle gate in the tree boundary. Go ahead along the edge of the next large field, then between houses to the B4380 opposite The Wingfield Arms in Montford Bridge. Turn right along the pavement opposite, soon crossing the bridge over the river Severn.

Montford Bridge was an important crossing point of the river Severn on the coach route from London to Shrewsbury. Nearby Severn House was built in the 16thC by the original ford, serving as a hostelry for travellers and providing stables for horses. The toll house was built in 1637 near a wooden bridge over the river, which was later destroyed by floods. According to legend the famous outlaw Humphrey Kynaston evaded capture here, when his horse jumped across the deliberately part dismantled bridge. The current three arched bridge was the first one designed by Thomas Telford, the famous engineer. It was built of red sandstone from Nesscliffe Hill and opened in 1792, then widened in 1948. Since 1992 the A5 has bypassed the village.

2 Montford Bridge to Nesscliffe

6 miles

This section follows quiet country roads and field paths across timeless countryside, passing ancient churches and one of Shropshire's less well-known castles. Much of the route is shared with the Severn Way and Humphrey Kynaston Way, a new route for horseriders.

1 Beyond the former toll house turn left along a road signposted to Mountford, soon crossing over the A5. After just over ½ mile you reach the red sandstone St Chad's church in Montford. *Built in 1735-8 on the site of an earlier 13thC church it is the resting place for Charles Darwin's parents.* On the bend at the church entrance briefly bear left then turn right on the signposted bridleway/ Humphrey Kynaston Way along a stony track. When it bends down left keep ahead through a gate and follow a farm track along the field edge, then between high hedges. *This bridleway was once drover's route for taking cattle to the market.* Later, after a gate follow the track past Bridleway Cottage, then continue along a minor road to Shrawardine and a junction by St Mary's church. *Dating from 1213, it was largely rebuilt in 1649 after being damaged during the Civil War, then restored in 1893.*

On the right is Montford Parish Millennium Green containing the remains of the original motte and some later masonry of a once important border castle, first mentioned in 1165. It was one of two castles originally built on each side of a ford across the river Severn to protect this important crossing. In 1215 it was destroyed by Llewellyn Prince of Wales, rebuilt in stone in 1220 by Henry III, then transferred to the Fitz-Alan family in 1229 and renamed Castle Isabel. It probably then became more a fortified manor house. In 1583 it came under the ownership of Thomas Bromley, Lord Chancellor of England. In 1645 it succumbed to Parliamentary forces and was destroyed by fire. Sandstone was re-used elsewhere, including on defences in Shrewsbury.

2 Turn left along the road out of the village past The Courthouse – *the cellars of the original house were once used to keep prisoners* – and thatched

Welsh Bridge, Shrewsbury

tank onto a track by early 17thC Felton Butler Manor Farm. Follow it right through a gate, soon bending left past outbuildings, then turn right along the driveway. After gates bear left to a nearby road. Follow it past North Farm then later side roads to a major crossroad. Go down the road opposite towards Wilcott/Kinton, past a large timber-framed house then along a road on the right signposted to Kinton. Just past Greenacres turn right along another road by a bus shelter, past Queensway, a children's play area,

0 kilometres 1

0 miles ½

Nesscliffe Hill Country Park

Nesscliffe

Wilcott

Felton Butler Manor

Montford Bridge

Shrawardine

Montford

Steps. Go past a road on the left, then an entrance to a house/ farm on the right. Just after passing the Shrawardine road sign cross a stile on the right. Follow the stiled path along the edge of two fields, then north along the edge of a large field and down the next. Go half-right up the next field to its top corner, then continue along a track down towards farm buildings to a stile hidden behind a black water

then Kingsway and continue along Wilcott Avenue. Just before it bends half-right go through a kissing gate on the left. Follow the path along the field edge to another kissing gate and across a large modern suspension footbridge over the A5 dual-carriageway. Follow the undulating path to the road in Nesscliffe.

NESSCLIFFE TO LLANYMYNECH
13¾ miles

3 Nesscliffe to Melverley church
6¼ miles

The trail first passes through Nescliffe Countryside Heritage Site, a wooded hill containing the remains of an Iron Age fort, a legendary cave in its impressive red sandstone cliffs, and great views. It continues across farmland to the attractive hamlet of Kinton, then passes through a Military Training Area on a new proposed waymarked route described in paragraph 3, in process of being established in early 2016, to the historic 'Pott's Line'. After the temptation of the 18thC Royal Hill pub by the river Severn it continues to the rare early 15thC St Peter's church in Melverley.

Nesscliffe Countryside Heritage Site is a distinctive red sandstone hill covered in pines, tall redwoods and other unusual trees planted by the 6th Earl of Bradford. On its northern summit is an Iron Age hillfort that was occupied into the Roman period. For centuries the hill has provided stone for some of Shropshire's churches and castles. However it was once notorious as the place from where highwaymen would descend to rob merchants passing by on the important trading road between Shrewsbury and Oswestry. One of the most famous was 'Wild' Humphrey Kynaston (1468

-1534), the son of a local Lord. After falling into debt and being charged of murder, he became an outlaw and allegedly came to live in a cave in the cliffs here. Popular with the poor and feared by the rich he was eventually pardoned.

Turn left then after 15 yards cross the road to the former school with its clock. Go past its side, then follow a stiled path up the wood edge, then turn left along a signposted bridleway past a nearby sandstone quarry and across the wooded slope. Soon go up a path on the right to Kynaston's Cave and an information board. Turn right beneath the cliff face then follow a path up beside a wooden fence, passing above the quarry, and continuing by another fence through majestic Scots pines to a finger post. Continue ahead along the left of two paths through rhododendron and mature trees, soon bending half-right through an area of picnic tables to a finger post. Follow the path ahead signposted to Oliver's Point up into the site of the hillfort to a good viewpoint. The path now heads away, soon descending through more dense mixed woodland past an information board on the fort, where its ramparts are visible, and down to a finger post. Continue ahead past a bridleway leading left to Oak's car park. Follow the bridleway ahead, then take the signed Pines car park path through a small gate on the left and along the field edge to a road. Go down it. At the junction turn right through Hopton and keep ahead at the next.

2 Just beyond another junction take a signposted path through a gate on the left, Angle right across the large field to a stile in the first recessed corner. Go slightly right across the next field to a sleeper bridge/stile,

then angle left to a nearby boundary corner and continue beside it to a stile/gate. Follow the stiled path along the edge of the next two fields. Go briefly along the next field edge then through a gate on the left. Follow the path across the field to stile, then go ahead across the next large field for 100 yards to a hedge/tree boundary corner, then continue along the field edge to a road. Go along the road ahead over the A5, past Kinton Business Park entrance and on into Kinton. At the junction keep ahead past Kinton House and through the village. After passing a converted wood-clad tythe barn, next to a 16thC timber framed manor house, turn right along a stony track past nearby Kinton Grove to Castle Cottages. Continue down an enclosed green track to a kissing gate into Nesscliffe Military Training Area. *The Training Area was originally established during World War II as a Central Ammunition Depot by the*

MoD, serviced by new on site railway tracks. Since it closed in 1959 the site has been used by army and cadet personnel for training. No live firing takes place, but biannual exercises involve battle simulation charges, when access over public footpaths is controlled. Follow the new waymarked SW section.

3 Turn left along a green track just beyond, after a few yards bending right, then at a nearby track junction turn right towards a distant bunker in the trees. After a few yards at a nearby fence corner take a path angling left into and through the wood to a gate at its edge. Turn left along a stony track past mixed woodland, then a side track on the left, soon entering woodland. Just before the track splits take a waymarked stiled path on the left through the wood into a field corner. Go along the field edge to a stile /gate by a track. Follow the path

19

through the trees, then turn right along the former Potteries, Shrewsbury and North Wales railway, which opened in 1866, through the wood edge. *Known as the 'Pott's Line' it connected Shrewsbury with Llanymynech, and although beset with financial problems and several closures, it refused to die. In 1911 it was re-opened by Colonel Stephens, an eccentric railway man, who used a bizarre collection of second hand rolling stock, including railcars and former horse-drawn tramcars, designed for city streets! It then closed again in 1933, but in 1941 was restored by the Government as part of the development of the Ammunition Depot. It finally closed in 1960 and sadly little now remains.* Just beyond a footbridge/stile on the right near the wood corner, turn left down a path to a footbridge/stile, then go along the edge of a large field to cross two stiles. Go across the field to a gate, then half-right across the next to a partly hidden stile near the corner. Go across the next field to a gate and past a house, then go along a road past a 19thC Jubilee chapel.

4 Just after it bends left turn right along a short track to a stile. Turn left along the field edge to cross the facing of two stiles in the corner. Go across the field to a stile hidden in the tree boundary about 50 yards from the corner. Go slightly right through an area of young trees to a stile. Continue ahead past a private gate and on beside a fence to a road. Turn right then cross a stile on the left. Go across the field, through a gateway ahead, then go slightly right across

the next field to a stile/sleeper bridge in a recessed corner at the corner of a wood. Continue between the hedge and the wood. The designated route now goes through trees ahead to a stile in the corner of a caravan site, then continues to a road and turns left to a junction. An alternative is to turn left through the caravan site to its entrance by the Royal Hill pub then continue along the road to the junction. Follow the road signposted to Melverley and Welshpool. After just over ½ mile the road bends past a side road and continues past houses. Soon after passing Upper Bank, as the road bends half-right cross a stile on the left. Go across three fields to a road. Cross the stile opposite and go along the field edge to a stile and another ahead. Cross the former railway line to a nearby stile, then go half-left across the large field to a stile onto a road junction in Melverley – *a stopping place on the 'Potts Line'.* Go along the road ahead signposted to Melverley Church

The black and white timber-framed St Peter's church on the banks of the river Vyrnwy is one of the oldest of its type in Shropshire. Its churchyard contains two yew trees over 400 years old and its interior a Saxon font from an earlier church, early 18thC pews, a Jacobean altar and pulpit, a 18thC lectern holding a chained bible, and panelling dated 1588. The original church was burned by Owain Glyndŵr in 1401 during his uprising against the English and rebuilt in 1406. It is a rare example of a British church built from timber, wattle and daub, using local oak and pegged throughout.

4 Melverley church to Llanymynech

7½ miles

This peaceful section of the Shropshire Way follows the River Vyrnwy as it meanders through farmland almost to Llanymynech. For most of the way it goes along a flood defence embankment, known as 'The Argie' and you are likely to have most of it to yourself.

Go along an enclosed path to a ladder-stile, then turn left along a track to a stile/gate by the former water mill and Mill House. At a waymarked path junction keep ahead past the old mill and through a gate ahead. Just beyond bear right across open ground, down a gully and up to a stile. Go along the field edge briefly by the river Morda, then go to a stile on the embankment ahead. Follow the gated embanked path to a cross-track. Continue along the embankment through further gates.

2 Later, where the embankment splits, with power cables about 200 yards ahead of you, ignore the one leading half-right to gates but follow the other on the left by trees to a hidden stile and a large footbridge over a stream to a kissing gate. Go along the embankment, under the power cables to a stile. Go along the next field's riverside edge to a stile. Continue beside the river, and as it bends left

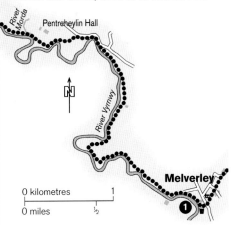

1 Go along the churchyard wall to a small gate, then past the caravan and camping site to a stile. Continue with the stiled/gated embanked waymarked path as it follows the meandering river through farmland. Later it continues by a fence above a road to a stile/gate just beyond a house. Follow the stiled/gated embanked path curving round the field edge, then westwards – *with a view of nearby 18thC Pentreheylin Hall* – and continuing away from the river to houses. Ignore a private stile ahead and cross a stile to your right.

keep ahead to a stile. Go along the field and under power cables then go half-right past the tree boundary corner and on across the field to pass through an

21

River Vyrnwy

old hedge/tree boundary. Just beyond turn left along a short track through a gap, then go along the left-hand riverside edge of a large field, past a telegraph pole, to a waymarked gap in the corner and over a stream. Go along the left-hand edge of another three large fields, whose vegetation and trees hide the nearby river in summer.

3 Before the final corner bend right along the field edge, then right again before the next corner to go through an old gateway in the hedge boundary passed through earlier about 40 yards from the corner. Go half-left across the next field corner to follow a short green track through a wide gap in the boundary. Go along the left field edge, with the river now visible below, then bend right for a few yards, then left through a waymarked gate into the adjoining field. Keep ahead along its left-hand edge and through a gateway in the tree boundary. Angle a third left across the next large field aiming for two distant telegraph poles to the right of a large house, past a tree boundary corner to a gate ahead. Here turn right through another gate then left up the middle of the narrow field

to the B4398 opposite a farm. Cross the road and follow it left, shortly joining a pavement, into Llanymynech. Continue to crossroads at the A483 by the Cross Keys Hotel.

Llanymynech straddles the border between Shropshire and Powys, and lies on the course of 8thC Offa's Dyke, which marked the kingdom of Mercia. Its earliest settlement dates to the Iron Age, when a fort, one of the largest in Britain, was built on the top of Llanymynech Hill. Its mineral deposits of copper and lead have been mined since the Roman period and probably earlier. It is though its abundant limestone deposits that have had a major impact on the area. With the opening of the Ellesmere Canal in 1796 large scale lime production began. Limestone was quarried then burned in kilns, using coal from Oswestry and Chirk areas to make lime primarily for use as a fertiliser, but also for use in the iron industry. The arrival of the Llanfyllin branch of the Cambrian Railway in 1863 took trade away from the canal but greatly boosted the lime industry, until it ended in 1914. The quarries finally closed in the 1930s.

LLANYMYNECH TO LOWER FRANKTON
10¾ miles

This section follows the partially restored Montgomery Canal, with occasional information boards, to the Llangollen Canal at Lower Frankton. After a short length of restored canal you follow the disused dry canal past Pant for 2½ miles to Pryce's Bridge 84 – the current limit of the restored canal. Following the towpath along the remainder of the attractive navigable canal, often lined with trees and wildflowers, which attract dragonflies and butterflies, is a delight. The tranquil canal supports waterlillies and rare acquatic plants, and attracts otters and herons. The section is well served by refreshment stops – the tea-shop at Canal Central, the Navigation Inn at Maesbury Marsh or the Queens Head pub by the A5.

The Montgomery Canal ran 35 miles from the Llangollen Canal through north-west Shropshire, then Powys in eastern Wales, to Newtown. The section from Frankton Junction on the Llangollen Canal to just south of Llanymynech was built as a branch of the Ellesmere Canal in the mid 1790s (see page 33 for more information), primarily to carry limestone quarried at Llanymynech to canalside kilns, where it was burned to produce lime, primarily for fertiliser. The canal connected with the new Montgomeryshire Canal which extended south to Welshpool, finally reaching Newtown in 1819.

Other products transported by canal included timber, slate and lead. In the second half of the 19thC, when the canal was then part of the Shropshire Union canal system, trade gradually declined due to competition from the railways. It fell into disuse after it was breached in 1936 and was formally closed in 1944. Since 1969 sections of the canal have gradually been restored by a partnership of volunteers, statutory and voluntary bodies. It is currently navigable in three separate sections.

5 Llanymynech to Queens Head
6¾ miles

From the Cross Keys Hotel walk north along the pavement beside the A483. then descend steps to the Montgomery Canal. Turn right along the towpath. All too soon this restored section of canal ends. For the next 2½ miles you walk alongside the disused canal, lost to nature but quite discernible, passing under a few bridges, with an information board at bridge 88. The former towpath is easy to follow, with the early section generally on a wide embankment that passes through intermittent woodland. Eventually you pass under Pryce's bridge 84 and walk past a wide section of restored canal, which opened in

23

Montgomery Canal, Llanymynech

July 2014. Continue along the towpath, later passing under bridge 82, where there is another information board, then past moored narrowboats near road lift bridge 81.

2 Shortly you pass Canal Central – accessed from bridge 80 – *offering a shop, tea-room and accommodation. Horse drawn boat trips are available from here.* Continue with the towpath

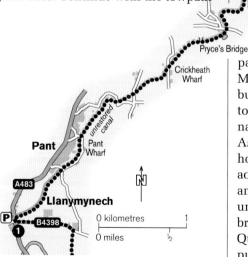

past the 18thC Navigation inn at Maesbury Marsh, which was once a busy inland port supplying Oswestry, to Aston lock no. 3, then follow a narrow green canalside track past Aston locks no. 2 to the former lock house. Follow its stony canalside access track past Aston lock no.1 and an information board. After passing under 76A follow the towpath under bridge 76 at the small community of Queens Head, named after its nearby pub. *Large warehouses were built here.*

Frankton Lock

6 Queens Head to Lower Frankton

4 miles

Continue along the straight section of canal then go under bridge 74, cross it, then descend beneath Heath House to continue with the towpath along the left side of the canal passing under the railway bridge. It crosses a small swing bridge by the disused Rednal Basin, which once provided a link with the railway, and later a small modern aqueduct over the river Perry. After passing the Graham Palmer lock – *a new shallow lock named after the founder of the Waterway Recovery Group* – it passes under bridge 70 near the junction with the Weston Branch – *which headed towards Shrewsbury but was never completed, and is now a nature reserve.* Continue past Frankton locks to reach the junction with the Llangollen Canal at Lower Frankton. Bend left along the towpath to a seat by bridge 1W.

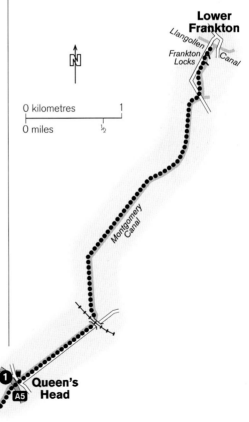

Lower Frankton

Llangollen

Frankton Locks

Canal

0 kilometres 1

0 miles ½

Montgomery Canal

Queen's Head

A5

25

LLANYMYNECH TO CHIRK BANK
18 miles

7 Llanymynech to Candy Woods
7½ miles

This well waymarked section is partly shared with the Offa's Dyke Path (ODP). It first visits the fascinating Llanymynech Lime Works Heritage site, with its Hoffman kiln, one of only three remaining in the country, then crosses the fomer quarry on Llanymynech Hill, now Llanymynech Rocks Nature Reserve. It then heads northwards along the wooded escarpment, initially with the ODP, then passes through Llynclys Common Nature Reserve, a limestone hill of woodland, meadows, and scrub, before descending to the road near Llynclys. From Dolgoch Quarry Nature Reserve it continues across undulating countryside via Sweeney Fen Nature Reserve to Trefonen, with its traditional Barley Mow Inn and small brewery. Here you rejoin the ODP continuing north to Candy Woods.

From the Cross Keys Hotel continue north along the road and cross the bridge over the canal, then turn right down a road past information boards. Turn left to another information board at the end of a car park. Turn right along a wide path past an old arm of the canal, soon bending left and passing the former lime works stables. At a path junction, either continue ahead on the Shropshire Way or better, turn right past an information board, then take the left fork to pass beneath a pair of vertical shaft draw kilns – *built in the 1870s* – then go up steps to the Hoffman kiln, which replaced them in 1900. *The kiln, with 14 chambers and tall chimney, was able to burn lime on a continuous basis.* Go past the left-hand side of the kiln and follow a path ahead through trees to a path junction/information board. *Here were once three tramways, from which stone was brought down to the respective kilns from the Tally House.* Turn left to pass through the earlier tramway to rejoin the Shropshire Way. Turn right past the ruined Tally House. After crossing the stream take the narrow path's left fork to pass through a short tunnel. The path rises through the edge of trees, then bends left to a path junction. Ignore the small gate ahead but turn right up the former gravity balanced incline through trees to a kissing gate and on up to the English brake drum house. At the cross-path beyond turn left and follow the stony path through the former quarry. *It was worked from the early 19thC until 1918, and is now Llanymynech Rocks Nature Reserve.* At a kissing gate you join the Offa's Dyke Path. Follow the path to a nearby information board by the Welsh brake drumhouse. Turn left along the now shared path. Soon divert left to a seat at the 'Border Viewpoint'.

2 Continue with the waymarked path, soon rising gently across the hillside to a kissing gate. It continues up beneath the limestone cliffs to a small gate and on past woodland to leave the Reserve. The waymarked path continues near the golf course, later emerging from the trees and passing along the course's edge. After about 100 yards, the path turns left beside the wood, then through it to a stile, after which it descends in stages to a finger post at a crossroad of paths. Here you leave the ODP and go up the waymarked Shropshire Way (SW)ahead. It continues through the wood past two good viewpoints at the top of the cliffs, then descends railed steps, known as 'Jacob's Ladder', to enter Llynclys Common Nature Reserve – *a limestone hill of woodland, meadows, and scrub.* Continue down through trees, then follow the waymarked SW left fork through the wood, on to a kissing gate, through a clearing and on to gates. Follow the path ahead briefly through trees, across open ground past side paths, then along the edge of woodland and over a cross-path. Shortly the path descends through trees to a kissing gate and the bend of a stony track beyond. Turn left down a wide path, then take the waymarked SW left fork. Soon go down the right fork. At a path T-junction turn right and at a waymarked bridleway/path junction bend left with the bridleway down through the wood past side paths to a road. Turn left down it to the A495 near Llynclys. Turn right along the pavement opposite.

3 Turn left opposite a lay-by along a stony track past houses and over a disused railway line to a kissing gate into Dolgoch Quarry Nature Reserve. Follow the path briefly along the wood edge, then turn right to a kissing

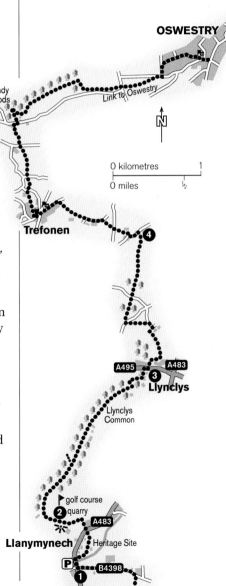

OSWESTRY

Candy Woods

Link To Oswestry

N

0 kilometres 1

0 miles ½

Trefonen

4

A495 A483

3

Llynclys

Llynclys Common

golf course

2 quarry

A483

Llanymynech Heritage Site

P B4398

1

gate into a field corner. Follow a path through the field to a gate at a farm complex. Turn left along the stony track to a gate by the last outbuilding back into the field. Go up its edge, through a corner gap and follow the path up the next field to go through a gap in the hedge. Turn right along the field edge to a road by Little Nut Tree Farm. Turn left along the road, then cross a stile on the left. Go across a large field and through a small wood to another road. Turn right to a kissing gate on the bend into Sweeney Fen. *This small reserve, described as 'the most exquisite flower meadow in Shropshire', is particularly known for its orchids.* Turn left to another kissing gate then right along the edge of the next large field into a wood. Follow the sunken path past sandstone outcrops and through trees to a ladder-stile. Go along the embankment to gate onto a road. Turn left, then right past the side of the house and on through woodland to a stile. Follow the boundary on the left along a narrowing field edge, shortly bending half-left with it along a narrow grass shelf to a kissing gate. Go along the next field edge to a nearby kissing gate and follow the boundary on your right. At the fence corner keep ahead past a nearby house to a kissing gate in the corner. Follow a faint green track along the field edge round to a kissing gate in the corner.

4 Turn left along the road, then right through the entrance to Gronwen Farm, and cross a stile on the left. Follow the fence by the access track, then angle left past the end of a hedge and on to a stile ahead. Go across the next field to a stile/gate onto a road. Cross the stile opposite and continue ahead beside the wooden fence – *with a view of ivy-covered Woodhill* – to a stile/gate into mature trees. Cross the stony track to a hidden stile just beyond a gate ahead onto Woodhill's driveway. Turn left, then bend right past outbuildings and continue up the narrow road. When it bends left at a finger post follow the bridleway slightly left ahead across open ground, through trees, to a waymark post. Descend through trees to another post and follow the bridleway briefly down beside the boundary, then angle left down through gorse to a bridle gate. Go across the rough field, over a stream and through a bridle gate ahead. Go up the field edge to another bridle gate, past garages and houses, then turn left along a road into Trefonen past a school and a church to a Pelican crossing on Oswestry Road. *Nearby is the 18thC Barley Mow Inn and adjoining Offa's Dyke Brewery. Trefonwen lies in the designated Oswestry Uplands on the line of Offa's Dyke. Despite its farming roots, the village was once a thriving industrial community, engaged in coal mining until 1891 and the quarrying of local limestone. It also had brickworks and a pottery.*

5 Go up Bellan Lane, soon rejoining the ODP by turning right along Malthouse Lane. Soon take the signposted hedge-lined bridleway/ODP ahead, then past houses and along a stony access track to a road. Cross a stile ahead and another nearby, then angle past a tree to the right-hand field boundary. Go up the field edge to a stile/gate. Turn left along the road, then right over a stile. Go along the long field edge to a stile in its recessed corner. Turn right a few yards, then left up the edge of two fields beside a section of Offa's Dyke, then along the next field to a road. Turn left, then right down the steep road towards Candy, at the bottom passing the Old Mill. At the junction turn right and after crossing the stream turn sharp left along a road past Brook Cottage and the driveway to Glan-yr-afon. Just past the house take the waymarked path rising steadily through Candy Wood to a crossroad of paths.

Link to Oswestry *(2½ miles)*

Turn right along the wide level path, shortly bending left and passing above a house and through more open woodland, then go up a stony track. Follow it past a stone building and on to pass behind a house to a kissing gate. Follow a faint green track angling right then continuing through parkland to a waymarked gate in a wall. Go past the corner of the large old walled garden to a stile/gate ahead. Go through a small wood, soon bending right to a waymarked path junction. Turn right to a stile into a large field. Go along its edge, soon joining a green track, which bends left down and along the bottom of the large field to a road. Follow a faint track across the large field opposite. Shortly angle left past a small tree, then follow the boundary on your right to a road by Rose Cottage. Turn right, then soon left along a narrow road. At its end

turn right down Maserfield through a housing estate, later passing Oswald's Well. Continue along Oswald's Well Lane past Brynhafod playing field. At the T-junction turn left, over Welsh Walls, then take a walled signposted path to the Heritage Centre and nearby St Oswald's church in the centre of Oswestry.

8 Candy Woods to Selattyn Tower
5½ miles

The trail continues northwards with the Offa's Dyke Path, through Candy and Racecourse Woods to the historic Oswestry Racecourse. Soon afterwards the routes diverge, then rejoin to approach Selattyn Hill, where the Shropshire Way heads east to a 19thC tower on its summit (1220 ft/372 metres) offering panoramic views.

After a short steep climb through trees the ODP/SW reaches a wide cross-path. Turn right, then at a nearby path junction turn sharp left up the path. It rises in stages through Candy Woods, then continues to a signposted path junction. Turn right through a nearby old wall and follow the path up through trees, then beside a fence past a seat and through Racecourse Wood to a kissing-gate. Continue straight ahead past a double-headed horse stone sculpture to seats by the ruin of Oswestry Racecourse grandstand and an information board.
The 2 mile long figure of eight racecourse lies on a plateau about 1000 feet high. Racing began in

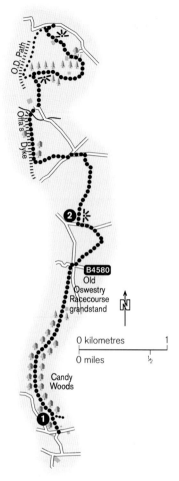

B4580
Old
Oswestry
Racecourse
grandstand

0 kilometres   1

0 miles   ½

Candy
Woods

the early 18thC, originally for local gentry and annual meetings became a popular event. The most famous race was for a silver cup donated by Sir Watkin William Wynn in 1777. The grandstand was built in 1804 at the start-finish line. Unfortunately, the recourse attracted notoriety due to heavy drinking, increasingly rowdy behaviour and petty crime, which led to falling attendances. The arrival of the railways made other racecourses more accessible and in 1848 the

last race was held and the course abandoned.

Continue north with the bridleway to staggered crossroads at the B4580, where you leave the ODP. Cross the road and follow the signposted SW rising steadily through Old Racecourse Common, then with a seat ahead, turn right to a finger post. Follow the narrow path down through trees, then go along a narrow green track. At a house cross a stile on the left and angle right to follow the waymarked path through the field to a road. Turn left up it past Pen-y-Rhos and Glopa Farm, then go through a gate on the right.

2 Go up the field to a large stone at a great viewpoint. Continue along the long field to cross a stile on your right. Go half-left across the field to a stile near the corner. Follow the boundary along the next field to a stile. Go down the next field edge, then cross a stile on the left by a gate. Angle right down across the sloping field to a stile. Go up the field edge to a stile, then turn left up the road. At a junction turn left, then go through a gate on the right. Follow the stiled path half-left across two fields then ahead up the large reedy field to the corner of high woodland to rejoin the ODP. Follow it along a section of tree-covered dyke, then along the edge of two fields and over a footbridge in a small dingle. Go up the short field and briefly along a nearby farm's access track, then turn left down another track to a stile/gate. Continue along the green track, soon rising, to a gate, then an enclosed path up to a stile/gate. Follow a rough green track up to a stile above a gate at a conifer corner. Here the Shropshire Way leaves the ODP for a short while, although it remains an option. Turn right past an unusual lift finger post and go along the edge of two fields by the plantation to a stile/gate. Angle right across the rough track through heather and small conifers to the Selattyn tower. *It was built in 1847 within an early Bronze Age ring-cairn at an important viewpoint, by a Mr Crewe, possibly as a commemorative folly to Prince Gwen, a 6thC prince, who was allegedly killed near here. An urn containing human remains was found at the time. In World War II it was manned by the Home Guard as an observation post.*

9 Selattyn Tower to Chirk Bank

5 miles

After rejoining the Offa's Dyke Path the route continues north, later featuring an impressive section of the 8thC earthwork, and a good view of Chirk Castle. It then leaves the Offa's Dyke Path for the last time, heading east along the wooded Ceiriog valley to share a section of the Maelor Way, later beside the river, to reach Chirk Bank. This small Shropshire village adjoins the Llangollen Canal and lies very close to the Welsh border. A short diversion along the canal takes you across Telford's aqueduct, now part of a World Heritage Site, into the small historic Welsh border town of Chirk.

From the tower the path descends to an information board and through heather to a kissing gate. Go down the edge of two fields to a kissing gate. Follow the restricted byway down the next field edge, then round to a kissing gate in the far corner. Follow the path along the bottom of the wood down to a stony track. Follow it left up to a wooden gate across it and go through the waymarked adjoining gate. Angle up the middle of the field to a gate in its top corner. Go across the next field to a stile in its right-hand corner. Follow the waymarked path through trees to a gate. Go along the field edge past a nearby house to a gate at a good viewpoint. Go down the field to a stile, then down the next field edge past the corner to turn right down a path to a stony track where you rejoin the Offa's Dyke Path. Go down the track and along a road, then turn left down the no through road to Bronygarth, soon bending past old limekilns, then rising to its end at Yew Tree Farm. Go past

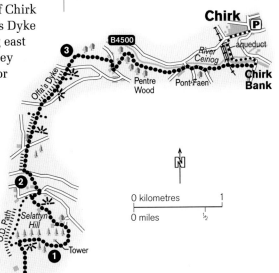

its side and up the initially narrow enclosed path ahead, then turn left up a road.

2 Just beyond Fairview cross a stile on the right and go up the edge of two fields to a road, then cross a stile opposite. Follow the next section of waymarked stiled ODP – *with a view of Chirk castle* – to a signposted crossroad of routes and down a field – *with a view now of Chirk* – then to a footbridge in a dingle and up to a gate. Go up the short field edge to a stile onto a lane. Turn right then cross the nearby stile. The ODP soon passes beneath the substantial tree-covered dyke, then continues along it – *now with a view down to Chirk viaduct and adjoining aqueduct* – down to an information board by a track. Cross the stile opposite and follow the tree-covered dyke down the field to a stile and on down to another by a house – *with a view of Chirk Castle ahead.*

3 Here you say farewell to the ODP by turning right on the waymarked Shropshire Way across the slope beneath a telegraph pole, then follow a path past the wood and on to adjoining telegraph poles to cross a stile beyond. Turn left down the field edge, through a gateway, then angle right down the field to a kissing gate onto a track. Turn left then right across a nearby stile. Go across the field to a waymarked gap in the tree boundary, then follow a path down towards a house to a wide waymarked gap in the boundary. Turn right to a stile/gate and go past The Old School. Go briefly along the road then turn left down a track, over a cross-track, to a house. Go through a waymarked gate ahead and down the enclosed path, then through trees to a kissing gate. The waymarked path now heads eastwards along the Ceriog valley into Pentre Wood, shortly descending to a large footbridge over a stream and continuing above the river. Go along the riverside edge of two fields, then follow a track through another field to a road at the hamlet of Pont-Faen. Go along the road ahead. At the junction turn right up the road, then left along a side road past Yew Tree cottages and on beneath woodland. Take the signposted SW angling left through mature woodland and across a steep wooded slope to a stile. Follow the stiled path between fences, along a field edge, then across the railway line. The path continues along the edge of a large field – *with Llangollen Canal visible below* – then bends right across to a small gate onto a track. Go through another opposite and along a hedged path down to a road at the small community of Chirk Bank. Turn right.

Link to Chirk centre *(1 mile)*

Go down the road, over the bridge, then follow the access lane beside the canal north to houses, then continue along the towpath and across the splendid aqueduct into Wales. With Chirk tunnel ahead take the wide pathway up to Castle Road. Follow it right to the B5070 opposite St Mary's church in Chirk.

CHIRK BANK TO ELLESMERE

9¾ miles

This is a delightful section of easy level walking, predominantly alongside the popular Llangollen Canal, to the small attractive town of Ellesmere.

The Llangollen Canal was originally part of the Ellesmere Canal, an ambitious but ultimately unsuccessful scheme to link the river Mersey, Dee and Severn rivers. Its aim was to establish a commercial waterway from Netherpool (Ellesmere Port) to Shrewsbury, serving the mineral industries of north east Wales, and the manufacturing centres of the West Midlands. Work started in 1795 under the guidance of renowned engineers Thomas Telford and William Jessop. By 1805 only part of the canal system had been completed: the northern section from the Mersey to Chester, a branch to Llanymynech, the main section to Trevor, including the major engineering feats of Pontcysyllte and Chirk aqueducts and Chirk tunnel, and most of the branch to Whitchurch. The plan to extend south through Wrexham to Trevor was abandoned due to financial and technical difficulties, as was the final 9 miles into Shrewsbury.

A new feeder canal was built connecting the Dee near Llangollen to Trevor Basin and the Whitchurch Branch was extended to join the Chester Canal at Hurleston, near Nantwich. The canal became part of the Shropshire Union Canal system in

1845. More recently this section has been renamed the Llangollen Canal, despite it not been included in the original plans!

Processed limestone from Froncysyllte was carried to the Midlands for use as flux in iron-smelting. Commercial traffic reached its peak in the mid-19thC, but had ceased by the late 1930s. The canal survived formal closure in 1944 mainly because it served as a conduit for moving fresh water from the Dee to Hurleston reservoir in south Cheshire. It has since developed into one of the most popular canals for holidaymakers in Britain.

10 Chirk Bank to Lower Frankton

6½ miles

Go up the road and turn left briefly along Oaklands Road, then go through a gate on the right into a large field. Go past the tree boundary corner ahead, then a waymarked post to a kissing gate ahead. Go across the next field to a stile in the hedge ahead just beyond its corner. Follow the embanked path through trees to another stile ahead. Go up the large field to a stile then across the next field to a stile near its left-hand corner. Go past the side and end of the building, then along a rough lane past houses to the road in Rhoswiel. Turn left to cross

33

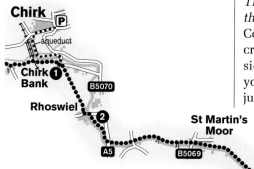

This traditional canalside pub faces the canal and not the adjoining A495. Continue along the towpath, then cross over bridge 3W to the opposite side. After passing under bridge 1W you reach a seat by Lower Frankton junction.

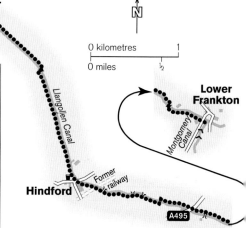

the bridge over the canal, then follow the signposted SW down to the canal towpath and under the road bridge (18W).

2 Continue along the tree-lined canal past a golf course, a small marina and a converted warehouse. Later, after passing under the B5069 road bridge 13 W at St Martin's Moor, not far from the former coalmining village of St Martin's, continue along a canalside narrow lane, then track. Cross bridge 12W and continue beside the canal past New Marton Top Lock by a cottage. *Lock Cottage on the opposite side sells ice cream & lollies.* Continue past New Marton bottom lock then along the narrow grass towpath to the Jack Mytton Inn at Hindford. *It is named after 'Mad' Jack Mytton (1796-1838) Shropshire's notorious local squire from Halston Hall, near Whittington. After inheriting a fortune he led a life devoted to racing, gambling, drinking and eccentric behaviour, before dying in a debtor's prison.* Later, cross bridge 6W and continue beside the canal past a narrowboat cruiser hiring business just before The Narrowboat pub, which is accessed from bridge 5W.

The original main route of the canal headed south for one mile along what is now the Montgomery canal then turned south east towards Shrewsbury. When this route was abandoned the planned branch to Whitchurch via Ellesmere became the main route to Chester.

11 Lower Frankton to The Square, Ellesmere
3¼ miles

The route continues across farmland then rejoins the canal, later following a short branch into Ellesmere, to reach the historic town centre beyond.

▌ Cross bridge 1W and continues up the road, then turn right along a No

Through Road. At the next junction turn left and follow the road up to its end at Oakwood to gates ahead into a field. Go half-right and follow the waymarked stiled path through several fields, then, at the boundary of a house, left round the field edge. Cross two forks of the house's driveway and follow the narrow waymarked path ahead between boundaries to a kissing gate to rejoin the canal.

2 Go under bridge 63 and continue along the towpath passing under further bridges to reach a junction of the canal, where the main branch continues east towards Hurleston. *The nearby imposing Beech House was built in 1805 as the Ellesmere Canal Company head office. It contained a corner committee room on the ground floor, designed to overlook the three arms of the canal. It is reputed that Thomas Telford stayed here during the construction of the canal. Adjoining the house was a maintenance yard, containing a dry dock and workshops. It is still used today by the Canal and River Trust.* Bear left under bridge 59 and continue along the short arm of the canal to its end at Ellesmere Wharf. Angle right then continue along Wharf Road. At the T-junction by the Black Lion Hotel turn right to the The Square in the town centre by Cross St/High St

and the old town hall – *built in 1833. Ellesmere is a small attractive old market town of Saxon origin, lying near The Mere, the largest of nine glacial meres in the area. Roger de Montgomery, Earl of Shrewsbury built a motte and bailey castle here after 1086. Afterwards its ownership changed many times and it was abandoned in the 14thC. The town developed around the castle and St. Mary's church and was granted a charter by Henry III in 1221 to hold weekly markets. The town's prosperity was enhanced later for a while by the opening of the Ellesmere Canal, then a railway in the 1860s connecting it with Oswestry and Whitchurch. Nowadays, its interesting buildings and beautiful lake attract many visitors each year.*

35

ELLESMERE TO WHITCHURCH

14½ miles

The Shropshire Way continues across low lying countryside, featuring meres, canals and Fenn's, Whixall and Bettisfield Mosses National Nature Reserve. This section then continues along the Llangollen Canal, not designated as part of the Shropshire Way network, to enable the inclusion in the circuit of the historic market town of Whitchurch and the attractive links to it. For those wishing to go directly to Wem, I have also described the link section to Welsh End junction.

with Love Lane go up the road ahead. At Rosebank turn left up the stepped path to a kissing gate into Castlefields Meadow - the site of the motte and bailey castle. Follow the path ahead – *soon with a view of The Mere* – down to a chained rock sculpture. Bend right with the path, soon taking the left fork past another sculpture down towards the lake. At a crossroad of paths turn left to a kissing gate by the road. *Nearby is The Boathouse café and*

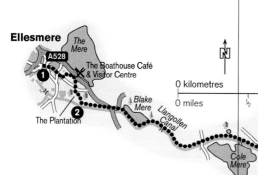

12 Ellesmere to Bettisfield

5¼ miles

The trail first heads to The Mere, passes through a small nature reserve, then resumes its journey along the part tree-lined canal past Blake and Cole Meres, later briefly passing through Wales around Bettisfield.

▌Continue along High Street. At crossroads go up St John's Hill ahead, past side roads. At a junction

Visitor Centre, with its delightful lakeside garden. Here turn right along a surfaced path up to a kissing gate. Just beyond take the waymarked SW grass path angling right up the slope and on near a fence to kissing gates at a lane into the Plantation Nature Reserve opposite. Go up the stepped path, then take the waymarked right fork through trees down to another path junction. Turn left along the bottom wood edge, past side paths, to an information board, then continue by a wooden fence to the canal.

2 Turn left along the surfaced towpath, shortly passing through Ellesmere Tunnel – *80 metres long with a railed towpath.* If lucky you might be accompanied by a boat passing through with its pilot light on. Continue along an attractive section of the canal past Blake Mere. After bridge 56 the towpath becomes more uneven, then grassy. The canal passes Cole Mere, with glimpses of it through adjoining Yell Wood. *The beautiful lake, surrounded mainly by woodland, with two flower-rich meadows, supports a range of wildlife. It is the only site in England containing the rare Least Water Lily. It is an SSSI and managed as a Local Nature Reserve. Bridge 54 gives access to an information board outlining a circular route from here.* The canal then bends north past Lyneal Wharf – *a canal based holiday centre for people with disabilities* – and continues under further bridges, later passing Bettisfield – *recorded in the Domesday Book in 1086. The oldest surviving building is 16thC Bettisfield Hall just to the north. The small rural border settlement later found itself on two major transport corridors, with the building of the canal in 1797 and the Whitchurch–Ellesmere–Oswestry railway. A station, with sidings, ¼ mile to the north of here, opened in 1863. It handled local traffic, while longer distance trains used a passing loop. During both World Wars the station was busy serving army camps at Bettisfield Park. The line closed in 1965.*

13 Bettisfield to Whixall Marl Allotment
3¾ miles

The Shropshire Way soon diverts from the Llangollen Canal to visit Bettisfield Moss, then returns to the canal via a short section of the Prees Branch, before visiting Whixall Moss.

Fenn's, Whixall and Bettisfield Mosses National Nature Reserve, an SSSI, straddles the border of England and Wales. It is the third largest lowland raised peat bog in Britain. Rescued in 1990 by the Nature Conservancy Council from destruction by large-scale commercial mechanical peat-cutting and drainage, it has been intensively restored and is now an internationally recognised habitat for bog plants and wildlife, some rare. Among those now thriving are butterflies, moths, dragonflies, adders, common lizards, and wetland birds. Peat had been cut in the Mosses primarily as fuel for domestic use since at least the 16thC, but it was the arrival of the canal, then the railways, providing an accessible means of transporting the peat to markets, that greatly increased the scale of activity.

A well as hosting firing ranges Whixall Moss was a top secret strategic World War II Starfish Site, where 65 fire baskets would be lit as a 'burning town' decoy to divert German bombers from Liverpool and Manchester. The site has been reconstructed as part of a history nature trail. Whixall's peat has also revealed three well preserved bodies, dating from the Bronze Age.

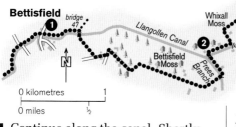

Bettisfield
bridge 47
Llangollen Canal
Bettisfield Moss
Whixall Moss
Marl Allotment
Prees Branch

0 kilometres 1
0 miles ½

I Continue along the canal. Shortly, cross bridge 47, then follow a waymarked path across three fields to a road. Follow it left. At a junction turn left along a rougher road, soon bending right, then continue along the right of two stony tracks past Moss Poldings to its end by other houses. Continue ahead along a wide tree-lined path past a small wood then turn left to a kissing gate into Bettisfield Moss. Follow the path past an information board and on along the edge of the Reserve. Shortly, the waymarked SW bends right and initially follows a faint green track through woodland, then continues along the woodland edge to another information board at the Reserve corner. Follow a path ahead through bracken and trees, then go along a stony access track to Brookhouse. Here turn left along a track past a barn, then angle across a field to a gate in its right-hand corner by a house. Note the line of the canal ahead raised above field level. Cross the nearby lift bridge over the Prees Branch of the Llangollen Canal. *Ironically the Prees Branch never actually reached its intended destination. It is navigable to Wixhall marina, then becomes a nature reserve.* Turn left along the towpath to reach the Wixhall Moss junction with the Llangollen Canal. Cross bridge 46 – *a roving bridge that allowed horses*

towing laden canal boats to cross the canal, when the towing path changed sides, without needing to be unhitched.

2 Go under the bridge and continue along the towpath. At a Wixall Moss information board by a lift bridge turn left past a car park. Continue ahead past Deepdale and along a green track past an information board on Albert Allmark's peat mill. Go through a facing gate at a Reserve Welcome Board and on between woodland. At a crossroad of green tracks turn right and follow the waymarked SW east across the expansive moss to eventually reach a track T-junction. Turn right down through two gates to leave the Reserve. Go through a small gate on the left and follow a short section of the Mosses Trail round to an information board on Wixall Marl Allotment – *a very rare surviving example of common land used for rough grazing and for exploiting marl, a crumbly limestone clay used as fertilizer* – and a gate onto a stony canalside track.

14 Whixall Marl Allotment to Welsh End junction
1¼ miles

A short Shropshire Way link to section 17 leading to Wem.

I Turn right along the track then cross bridge 44 over the canal and go through a kissing gate ahead. Go across two fields, along the next field edge, through a corner hedge gap and on across another field to a road. Follow it left past Wixhall Primary School, then a side road. At the next junction turn right signposted to Bostock Hall/Wem. Shortly cross a stile on the left then go across the field and through a gate in its right-hand corner. Just beyond go half-left up the large field to follow its boundary on your right to go through a waymarked gate in its far corner into another field at the junction of two Shropshire Way sections.

15 Whixall Marl Allotment to the town clock, Whitchurch

5½ miles

This section continues along the Llangollen Canal to rejoin the official Shropshire Way at the former Whitchurch Branch. After a short restored section it follows the route of the former canal arm, now a delightful green corridor into the heart of Whitchurch.

1 Turn left along the stony access track adjoining the canal screened by trees. When it bends left rejoin the canal and continue along the grass towpath. It passes under a series of bridges, an area of moored residential boats between lift bridges, Whitchurch Marina, then under A41 bridge 31A. Shortly the canal splits and meets the Sandstone Trail. A Shropshire Way link continues along the towpath of the main canal to end at Grindley Brook, with its impressive flight of staircase locks.

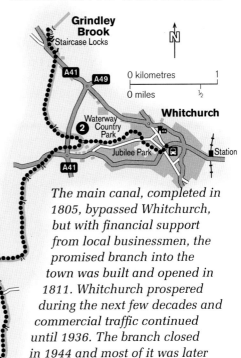

The main canal, completed in 1805, bypassed Whitchurch, but with financial support from local businessmen, the promised branch into the town was built and opened in 1811. Whitchurch prospered during the next few decades and commercial traffic continued until 1936. The branch closed in 1944 and most of it was later sold and partly built over. A short section from the junction was restored in 1993 and there are plans to extend into a new canal basin.

2 Cross lift bridge 31 and walk beside the short navigable section of the Whitchurch Branch of the canal to Chemistry Bridge – *the only surviving original bridge.* Continue along a stony path, under a bridge, and on to a finger post at a road. Angle left to another finger post, descend steps and follow the stony path to an information board. Turn right along the path signposted to the 'Town' through Whitchurch Waterway Country Park, over a minor road then past houses, and on to a mini roundabout. Cross the road and bear left through Sherrymill Hill car park to an arched gateway. Continue through Jubilee Park, with its bandstand, then along a path, soon enclosed, passing The Old Mill hotel/bar/restaurant – *the former steam-powered corn mill built in 1826 near the canal basin, now Brookes Court* – to reach Mill Street. Turn left to a mini-roundabout at an area known as the Bullring – *where bull baiting once took place.* Go along a pedestrianised street opposite past the Star Hotel to the town clock.

Town clock, Whitchurch

WHITCHURCH TO WEM

13 miles

Whitchurch stands on the site of the Roman fort Mediolanum – 'the place in the middle of the plain', a days march between Chester (Deva) and Wroxeter (Diroconium). In Saxon times the small settlement was called Westhune and developed around a church built in 912 AD. After the Norman Conquest a motte and bailey castle was built here and the church replaced by one made of white Grinshill stone, after which the settlement became known as Whitchurch. The separate township of Dodtune, became integrated into Whitchurch and known as Dodington. The town steadily developed and was granted market status in the 14thC, becoming the trading centre for the surrounding agricultural area. It also became known for its leatherworking and shoe-making. After the completion of the canal in 1811 the town became a major collection and distribution centre for the popular Cheshire cheese. It was transported weekly by boat, taking two days, to Ellesmere Port, then sent to Liverpool for further distribution. During the 20thC the town held regular cheese fairs and the tradition of local cheese-making remains today. The town further prospered with the arrival of the Crewe-Shrewsbury railway in 1858, and the railway to Oswestry in 1863. Whitchurch is also renowned for its clock-making tradition. The most famous is the J B Joyce & Co. reputed to be the oldest clock manufacturer in the world. The family business was first established around 1690 in the village of Cockshut, then moved to Whitchurch in 1790. Over the years the company made large mechanical clocks for churches, public buildings, railway stations in Britain and around the world. In 1964 when the last member of the Joyce family retired, the company was taken over by Smith of Derby. The iconic company building on Station Road, where turret clocks were made, is now an antique auction house.

16 Whitchurch to Welsh End junction
8½ miles

The Shropshire Way heads out of Whitchurch to visit Brown Moss Nature Reserve, then passes the tempting truck stop cafes adjoining the A41. After exploring Prees Heath Common Reserve, which has a fascinating history, and is home to the rare silver-studded blue butterfly, it continues west to the junction of SW routes at Welsh End.

I From the town clock return along the pedestrianised street to the mini-roundabout, then turn left along Watergate and up Dodington, past attractive 16thC timber-framed buildings. After passing the

Almshouses cross Bridgewater Street and continue along the pavement past Rosemary Lane, then use a pedestrian crossing to the opposite side. Continue along the pavement past Dodington Lodge Hotel to the main road. Go along Edgeley Road opposite out of Whitchurch, under a railway bridge, to its end at houses. Follow the former road to the nearby A525. Cross with care and go along Edgeley Bank road opposite. After nearly ¼ mile go through a bridle gate on the left into a field. Follow the bridleway ahead beside the hedge, at its corner angling right to a small gate, then along the next large field edge to a road. Follow it right, at a junction bending left. Shortly the road enters Brown Moss Nature Reserve. *Comprising woodland, heathland, marshes, small lakes, Brown Moss is rich in plants and wildlife.*

2 After emerging from the trees turn right to a kissing gate. Just beyond the waymarked SW turns left through the trees, crosses a footbridge, then bends left to a seat in an open area with a view of a lake ahead. Follow a path half-right, then at a path T-junction the waymarked SW turns right, passes through woodland, crosses a sleeper bridge and continues to a waymark post near the wood edge. Turn left through the wood, past a small tree-enclosed lake, and on to a short boardwalked path at the corner of the large lake. Continue along the lake's wooded edge to a kissing gate to rejoin the road. Follow it right. At a junction the signposted SW continues through trees ahead to a post then

follows a path along the field edge to the A41. Turn right then cross the dual carriageway to the Raven Hotel opposite. Go along the former main road through Prees Heath, past the Famous Midway Truck Stop café, Lynn's Raven café, nearby roundabout and a garage. Continue along the A49. Soon cross to the signposted SW opposite into Prees Heath Common. *Prees Heath Common, lying between the busy A49 and A41, former Roman roads, has an interesting history. In the Bronze Age this lowland sandy heath.was used as a burial site, then for centuries was an important public open space, used by local people exercising their rights for grazing animals. Later gypies, with their horse-draw wagons, were regular visitors here and horse races attracted crowds in the early 20th..But it has a darker side for it has also been used by different generations of troops. In the 13thC King John's army gathered here before invading Wales. In the Civil War it was the Royalist army. In World War I a large army trench warfare training camp covered the common, after which it was reinstated. In World War II it became an internment camp for foreign nationals, then a bomber training airfield. Afterwards much of the land was intensively farmed. In the 1990s the threat of a proposal to extract sand and gravel from the site led to a campaign to save the common. In 2006 Butterfly Conservation bought part of the common and work began to restore it.*

3 Follow the waymarked SW, shortly becoming a green track passing between a compound corner and the former RAF control tower, adorned with information boards. About 100 yards further the waymarked SW turns left along a path towards the busy A41, then bends away and continues through the Reserve, low heather-covered in August with a few trees. Later it bends right to an information board on stones. Just beyond turn right along a narrow green track, soon parallel with the nearby A49 and continuing north. Shortly, continue along a parallel wide path to the left of the track. After about 120 yards, a few yards beyond a waymark post, turn left and follow the waymarked path, soon through trees, to the A49. Cross to a stile opposite. Go along the edge of the long field, in the corner bending left to cross a stile/footbridge/stile. Go half-left through a field to a gate onto a road. Turn right, shortly crossing the railway line, then at Bridge Farm Cottage, take the left fork signposted to Wem. At the next junction turn right, then left along a nearby side road past houses.

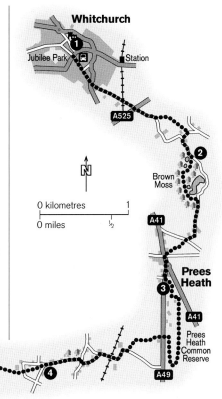

4 At The Woodland, when the road bends left, follow the signposted SW along a stony track ahead past Sandy Bank Kennels, then cross a stile on the left. Just beyond the tree ahead turn right across the field past a hedge corner to a stile in the corner. Go ahead through the next narrow field to a stile onto a road. Turn right, then cross a nearby stile on the left.

Go along the edge of two fields to a footbridge, then the left-hand edge of the next field. At a waymark post at the boundary corner, go slightly left to a stile in the right-hand corner. At Cumberland Cottage beyond turn right along its access track to a gate, then right along a stony track to the first house. Here go through a gate on the left and along a short enclosed path to a small gate. Turn left past the end of a barn to a small gate and along the field edge to a road. Follow it left through Hollingwood, then at the junction turn left, soon passing Cumberland Lane.

5 Just before a house take the signposted SW through a gate on the right. Turn left to a stile and on to another ahead. Go slightly right across the next field to a stile in the hedge before its corner. The path now angles left across the next field to a stile/gate. Go up the large field to a gate onto a road. Go up the road opposite past Millbank Farm to nearby Mill Bank Cottage, then follow the waymarked SW through a gate ahead. Walk beside the boundary, then at its corner continue ahead across the large field to a waymarked tree in its right-hand corner. Go slightly left across the next field to a hidden stile/sleeper bridge in the tree boundary. Go along the field edge to a stile/sleeper bridge/stile into the adjoining field at a junction of SW routes.

17 Welsh End junction to Wem

4½ miles

This section heads south through farmland on field paths and quiet country roads to Wem. It passes through the small village of Edstaston containing the remains of the Prees Branch canal and a gem of a small Norman church. In the main it is not newly waymarked until the outskirts of Wem, although some old SW waymarks remain.

Go ahead between a tree-enclosed pool and a hedge corner, then slightly right across the field to a stile. Follow the next field edge to a stile/gate. Go past a tree-enclosed pool and on across the field, over a farm track, and on to a stile/gate in the corner by the farm and Farthing Cottage. Cross

the driveway and follow the old hedge-lined restricted bridleway ahead to a road. Go along the road opposite through the scattered community of Whixhall, past Gilberts Lane by Braynes Hall Farm. At the next junction bend left past Greenacre Farm. Shortly, when it bends right, go along a waymarked short enclosed green track ahead to gates, then along the field edge to a stile in the tree boundary ahead. Continue along the next field edge past a tree-enclosed pool, then go half-left to a partly hidden stile in the tree boundary ahead. Follow the enclosed path, shortly passing a very long barn, to a wide tree-lined path junction. Continue ahead, shortly taking its right fork to a stile and on to a nearby farm's stony access track. Follow it right to gates, then continue along the driveway to a road. Follow it left through Edstaston, passing the village Hall, then The Wharf. *Here are the remains of the Prees Branch of the Ellesmere Canal, originally intended*

Brown Moss Nature Reserve

to link the river Severn at Shrewsbury with the river Mersey. *Unfortunately it ended at nearby Quina Brook and a wharf was built here to serve Wem, with goods brought by horse and cart.* Continue along the road to the lovely St Mary the Virgin's church. *Built around 1150 it was largely used as a chapel until 1850. Some of its original Norman features remain, along with 13th and 15thC wall paintings discovered in the 1970s. It is said that the playwright George Bernard Shaw attended the church on visits with his wife to see her family at nearby Edstaston House.*

2 At its entrance cross a stile opposite. Go along part thatched timber-framed White Lodge's access track to a stile into a large field. Go alongside the boundary and at its corner continue ahead across the field to a stile/gate. Go slightly right across the next large field, past a small tree-enclosed pool, and on to cross a stile in the protruding hedge boundary corner ahead. Go along the field edge and on across its corner to a stile ahead. Go slightly left across the next field to a stile and ahead along the edge of the large field to a kissing gate/gate in the corner onto a road. Turn left then immediately right along the road signposted to Loppington. Just past a small pond beyond a house, cross a stile on the left. Follow the stiled path in a straight line southwards across six fields then continue along the next field edge to a stile midway. Follow the enclosed gated path alongside two fields, then an enclosed surfaced path to a road in a housing estate in Wem. Turn left along a short enclosed pathway, then continue ahead along the road, soon bending right to a T-junction. Turn left past side roads to a main road. Follow a long enclosed straight path opposite to the High Street by the Castle Hotel.

WEM TO SHREWSBURY
13 miles

18 Wem to Grinshall
4½ miles

The Shropshire Way heads to the attractive village of Tilley, passes an unusual wartime school, then continues its journey south through farmland to the wooded escarpment famous for its quarried stone, above the attractive village of Grinshall.

Wem, derives its name from the Saxon 'Wamm', meaning marshland. In the Doomsday Book in 1086 the small settlement was held by William Pantulf. In the early 12th C the family built a motte and bailey castle near the current church of St Peter and St Paul, which dates from the 14thC. The castle's ownership subsequently passed to other families and by the late 15thC it had been abandoned. In 1202 King John granted the town the right to hold a weekly Sunday market. This was changed to Thursday in 1351 when Sunday markets were banned. In 1643 during the Civil War the small Parliamentary garrison of 40, said to be aided by women of the town, successfully withstood the attacks of around 5000 Cavaliers, led by Lord Capel. This led to the verse: 'The women of Wem and a few musketeers, beat Lord Capel and all his cavaliers'! In 1650 Sir Thomas Adam, born in Wem, a local landowner and former Lord Mayor of London, founded the

Adams Grammar School. In 1677 much of the town was destroyed by a fire accidently started by a young girl. Wem was largely an agricultural town, but it has a tradition of brewing dating to the 18thC, with many pubs brewing their own ale. In the 1890s brewing was consolidated into the Shrewsbury & Wem brewery. In 1987 the brewery closed. The town prospered after the arrival of the Crewe-Shrewsbury railway in 1858. Each year the town also celebrates Henry Eckford for his horticultural skills in cultivating the first modern sweet pea here.

Turn right along the High Street then left by the church along Mill Street (B5476). At the former Wem mill with its tall chimney – *dating from the early 19thC and powered in turn by water, steam then gas to ground corn into flour* – turn right and follow a narrow stony track near the river Roden to Mill Dam Cottage. Go through a kissing gate and along the field edge by the river round to another kissing gate. Turn left across the bridge over the river to a large gate then a smaller one ahead. Follow a path by a stream to a road. Follow it left through Tilley past old timber-framed houses and the 18thC Tilley Raven pub. At the junction go along the no through road ahead then cross the railway line with care. Follow a path left to a stile and across a field to a road. Go along the driveway opposite. When it splits keep ahead to a small gate by Pankeymoor Cottage. The path now follows telegraph poles across the field to ponds and a road, then continues across a field to another road.

2 Go through a kissing gate opposite and another ahead. Go half-left across the next field corner to a kissing gate. (The next section passes through a very large crop field. The wide cut path described ran further east than shown on the OS map, and may differ each year.) Follow the path ahead up the large field to pass nearby Woodlands School. *This Special Needs School is based in the former Trench Hall, built in the late 19thC for wealthy landowners, but best known for its use during the Second World War. In 1933 Anna Essinger, a prominent German Jewish educator came to Kent with a group of Jewish children to escape Hitler's harsh discriminatory educational regime and established a boarding school there. In 1940, when southern England became a defence area the school was forced to relocate to Trench Hall until 1946. Despite the inadequacy of the accommodation and limited financial support it provided a home and good education for exiled Jewish children, many of whom later had prominent careers.* At the school boundary corner/sports area angle left to a kissing gate in the hedge boundary corner ahead. Follow the kissing-gated path along the edge of three fields, then turn right along a wide hedge-lined green track. After about 150 yards turn left through a waymarked gateway into a field. Turn right to

a kissing gate and another beyond. Go along the field edge to a green cross-track and through a kissing gate opposite. Go across the field past a pool to a kissing gate, then along the edge of two fields to a road. Turn right a few yards into Clive. *Copper was mined here possibly from Roman times until the late 19thC.*

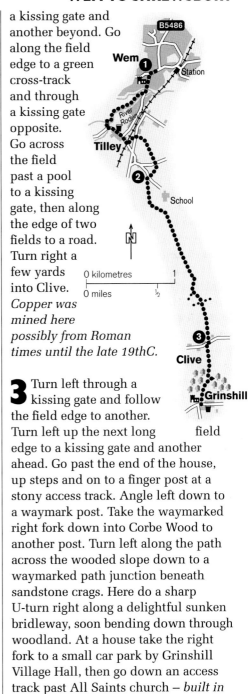

3 Turn left through a kissing gate and follow the field edge to another. Turn left up the next long edge to a kissing gate and another ahead. Go past the end of the house, up steps and on to a finger post at a stony access track. Angle left down to a waymark post. Take the waymarked right fork down into Corbe Wood to another post. Turn left along the path across the wooded slope down to a waymarked path junction beneath sandstone crags. Here do a sharp U-turn right along a delightful sunken bridleway, soon bending down through woodland. At a house take the right fork to a small car park by Grinshill Village Hall, then go down an access track past All Saints church – *built in*

47

1839-40 on the site of an earlier 11thC church – to the village road. This attractive village contains some old timber-framed houses, as well as the award-winning 'Inn at Grinshill' pub, but it is its high grade sandstone for which it is best known. The wooded escarpment above Grinshall has been quarried for sandstone, available in a range of colours, since the 12thC until the present day. It has been used in many Shropshire buildings, including Haughmond Abbey, the English and Welsh Bridges in Shrewsbury and its railway station, as well as further afield – even for the lintels and door surround of Number 10 Downing Street!

19 Grinshall to Abbey Wood car park, B5062
7½ miles

The Shropshire Way continues south through Hadnall and Astley villages to the substantial remains of Haughmond Abbey.

1 Turn right along the road, then left along Sandy Lane. Just after it bends half-right follow a narrow enclosed stiled path on the right past a house, then go across a field corner to a road opposite Three Cross Roads. Turn right then left through a nearby bridle gate. Follow the bridleway past the house and across two fields, then south along a wide track. After crossing a stream in a dip continue along an enclosed stony track to a road at the entrance to Sansaw Business Park. Turn left then at a kissing gate on the right take a path angling through the wood past

nearby business units and on to a small gate. Go across two fields into a wood. Follow the path past a nearby house, between boundaries and past a cottage – *with a view of the nearby converted 18thC windmill, known as The Round House* – to a stony track. Turn right then left through a kissing gate and go along the field edge to another kissing gate. Go across the next field to a kissing gate in its right-hand corner, then follow a path past gardens. After a side path the now narrow tree-lined path bends right to a kissing gate. Go ahead along the field edge to a road.

2 Go along Ladymas Lane opposite, then just before the bend, take a tree/hedge lined path on the left to a kissing gate into a large field. Follow the boundary on your right, then at its corner angle left across the field to a small gate and a kissing gate beyond by a small pool before a housing estate. Turn right across the small field, soon bending left to a bridle gate. Follow the enclosed path to a road. Turn left past Church Close, then just beyond turn right through a kissing gate. Take the path's right fork across the field, then go across the bowling club's car park to a road in Hadnall. Nearby is the New Inn. *Hadnall (Hadenhale) village was mentioned in the Doomsday Book of 1086. St Mary Magdalene church, dating from Norman times, was later restored and extended in the 1870s. Sir Rowland Hill, the Duke of Wellington's second-in-command at the Battle of Waterloo in 1815 was buried here.*

3 Turn right along the road, shortly crossing the railway line. When it bends right cross a stile on the left and follow the signposted SW angling down the field to its right-hand corner, over the railway line and across a narrow field to the A49. Cross with care then follow an enclosed path opposite to a lane. Follow the gated path through four fields and past a barn, then go along a stony track past the Village Hall to the road in Astley. Go along the road to St Mary's church. *Astley, recorded in the Doomsday Book in 1886, is now a peaceful village with several interesting old dwellings. St Mary's church, dating to the 12thC, was until 1860 a chapel to the Collegiate Church of St Mary in Shrewsbury. The tower was added in 1837. The main church bell dating to 1270, one of only a few bells in England cast before 1300, and possibly the oldest in Shropshire, was restored in 2012. In medieval times the area was partly administered by Haughmond Abbey.* Continue along the road out of the village, past nearby Astley House – *dating from the late 18thC but remodeled in Grecian Revival style around 1830* – and through Upper Astley to the A53 near The Dog in the Lane pub.

4 Turn right a few yards then cross the road with care down to gates. Follow the bridleway along the large field edge, then right along a hedge-lined green track to cross a stream at Wheatley Farm. Follow the stony track ahead between a horse training area and a large barn to gates. Go half-left to join a stony track bending through

a waymarked gate. Follow it along the field edge to gates. Here it bends left but continue ahead along a green track through a large field to a gate. Continue with the bridleway, soon beside a hedge, along a large field to a kissing gate. Go slightly left across the next large field past a woodland fence corner, then just before a kissing gate turn left up the field edge beside

New Coppice. Soon angle away from the wood to a kissing gate/gate in the left-hand corner. Go along the next field edge. *Hidden in the wood ahead is Iron Age Ebury Hillfort.* At a kissing gate/gate turn right along an unerringly straight hedge-lined old green lane, then go through sheep pens and along a track to Haughmond Farm. Go along its driveway and at the B5062 go through a kissing gate and follow the signposted path back across the field

49

to a ladder-stile into woodland. The path descends to a stony track, and continues down the edge of woodland – *with a great view of Haughmond Abbey below and distant Shrewsbury* – to a kissing gate. Continue to another kissing gate, then go long the field edge past the abbey round to its entrance. *Haughmond Abbey was founded in the early 12thC and was a thriving community until it was ended in 1539 by Henry VIII's Dissolution of the Monasteries. Afterwards the Abbey became owned by Sir Edward Littleton who converted the site into a private residence. After the Civil War the site was used for farming.* Follow the stony access track to the B5062. Turn left to nearby Abbey Wood car park.

20 Abbey Wood car park, B5062 to Shrewsbury

4½ miles

After passing through attractive woodland the Shropshire Way heads to Uffington. It then continues along a recreational route following the line of the disused Shrewsbury Canal, still evident in places, before following the river Severn to the English Bridge, giving access to Shrewsbury town centre.

1 Cross to the entrance to The Hollies opposite and follow the lower path through the attractive woodland. *Hidden nearby is Haughmond quarry, which has produced red sandstone*

50

for centuries and used to build Shrewsbury Castle and Abbey. At a waymarked path junction bend right along the edge of the wood. Just after passing under a pylon turn left along a path to a small gate/stile. Go across the field to cross a bridge over the disused Shrewsbury canal. Follow a green track to houses then a driveway to a nearby road opposite The Corbert Arms in Uffington. Turn right along the pavement opposite and just past Holy Trinity church – *dating from 1856 but founded in 1155* – turn left down Mill Lane. Go past a house to a view of the nearby river Severn, then past the other house. Follow a path up through trees to a kissing gate and across open ground to another. Turn left along a waymarked wide surfaced embanked tree-lined bridleway to pass under the A49. Continue with the tree enclosed bridleway past Pimley Manor and over a road to enter Old Shrewsbury Canal Countryside Site. Continue along the wide recreational route, later beside an attractive section of the old canal. (See page 55 for details.)

Shrewsbury / **Uffington**

0 kilometres 1

0 miles ½

2 At a signposted turning for Sundorne/Harlescot cycle/walkway turn left down a path through trees, soon bearing right across a stream to join the river Severn. Follow the path along the tree-lined riverbank and on through trees to pass under the A512 road bridge. Continue along a cycle free wide path near the river to the bend of a road. Go along the roadside verge by the river, then a surfaced path past seats overlooking the impressive weir. Continue along a wide cycle/walkway beside the river, passing under a footbridge, then the railway bridge to eventually reach the English Bridge. Go up steps to the road and turn right along and up Wyle Cop, over Dogpole, past St Julian's Centre, then along the High Street to The Square.

WEM TO ISOMBRIDGE FARM
16¼ miles

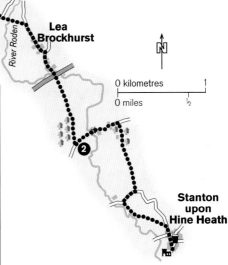

keep ahead to a kissing gate, then follow a path along a field edge to another kissing gate. Take the path's right fork through the next field to a footbridge over the river Roden

This is a section of a main route to Wellington, for an alternative Shropshire Way (North) finish, part of a continuous trail around Shropshire, or a day walk.

21 Wem to Stanton upon Hine Heath
6 miles

The route heads south east across farmland featuring the attractive ancient villages of Lee Brockhurst and Stanton upon Hine Heath, and an old byway.

I Follow the road east to the railway station. Cross the line then turn right along Aston Road past Orchard Way. After passing Cordwell Park turn right along a stony track signposted to Barker's Green. When it bends right and on past a house. Turn right up a lane, soon becoming a road. At the junction turn left. Just past the second house (Lothlorien) turn right along a signposted tree-lined bridleway. It continues through trees then bends left to Oakfields. Follow its access track to a road. Follow it right past a side road and the entrance to Brockhurst Farm. Just after Hillcop Bank Farm/boarding kennels, on the bend, go through a kissing gate. Descend the stepped path through trees then follow the path to a footbridge over a river, and through a field to a road. Follow it right through Lee Brockhurst – *an attractive village dating from Saxon times and containing 12thC St Peter's church, plus farms and buildings dating from the early 17thC.* Go across the sandstone bridge over the river Roden – *built about 1800 to carry the Shrewsbury–Whitchurch turnpike road* – to the A49 and up the restricted byway opposite. The delightful hedge-lined track makes a long gentle ascent to a wood then descends through trees, passing between sandstone outcrops. The narrow track then continues to a narrow track/road.

2 Turn left and follow the track over the river. When it bends right to a nearby house keep ahead up a sunken tree-lined sandstone track to the entrance to Papermill Cottage. Continue up the stony access track, then go through a kissing gate on the right and along a field edge to a stile. Follow the path down through the wood then continue ahead along a stony track. When it bends right to the house keep ahead alongside the large brick wall to a small gate. Go along the field/wood edge to another small gate. The path now angles left past a nearby tree, and across the large field towards another tree to a stile beyond. The path angles right across the middle of

the next large field to a stile by gates. Turn right along the high hedge-lined track. Just before it bends right cross a stile on the left. Go along the left-hand field edge then across the middle of a large field towards a house to a road. Follow it right into nearby Stanton upon Hine Heath. At a junction keep ahead through the village – *which once had a school and post office.* When the road bends left towards The Stanton Arms pub go along the road ahead signposted to Stanton Church. At the next junction continue ahead along Church Road to visit 12thC St Andrew's church.

22 Stanton upon Hine Heath to Poynton Green
5 miles

The trail continues across country to the scattered settlement of Muckleton, and the attractive hamlet of Great Wytheford to Poynton Green.

I Return along Church Road, then before the junction turn right along a lane past houses to a kissing gate. Go across the field to a small gate. Turn left along the large field edge to another small gate. Go along the edge of the next three fields, then descend through trees to a small gate/sleeper bridge and stile. Go up the field to a kissing gate and along a concrete track to Sowbach Farm, then follow its driveway to the A53. Cross a stile opposite and go slightly right across the large field to a stile at a signposted path junction. Turn left along the field edge past a large barn to a stile. Bear right along the next field to a house,

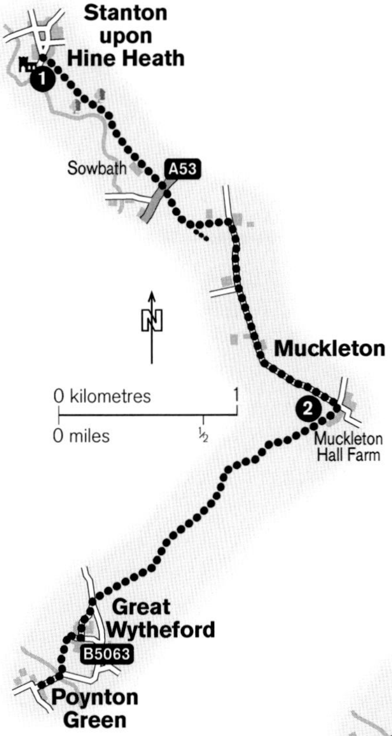

Stanton upon Hine Heath
Sowbath A53
Muckleton
0 kilometres 1
0 miles ½
Muckleton Hall Farm
Great Wytheford
B5063
Poynton Green

to the B5063. Follow another road opposite through Great Wytheford, past Wytheford House Farm, with its impressive large early 18thC house. On the bend turn right along an enclosed green track then cross a stile on the left. Go ahead along the field edge past mid 19thC Muckleton Hall Farm to a stile. Go half-left across the next field to a stile/sleeper bridge/stile, then along the nearby house's gravel driveway to a road. Follow it right across the river and on to a junction at Poynton Green.

23 Poynton Green to Isombridge Farm
5¼ miles

After passing an ancient farmhouse and chapel the route heads east to High Ercall, then continues to Isombridge Farm.

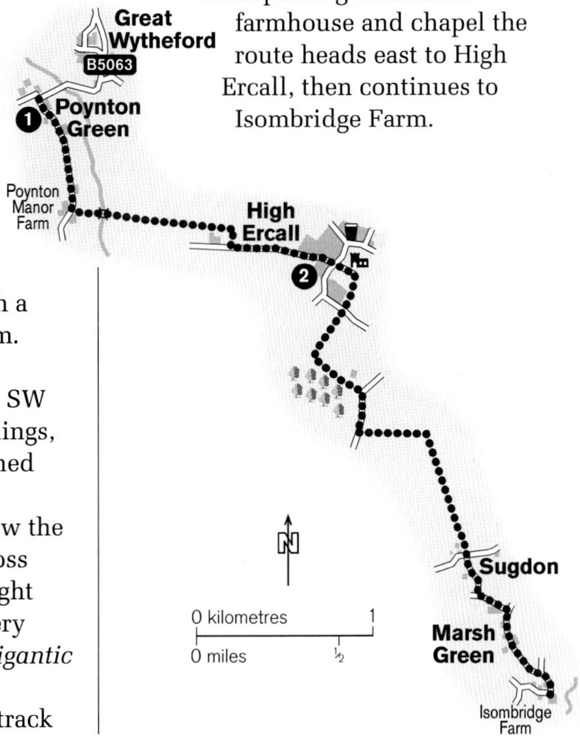

Great Wytheford
B5063
Poynton Green
Poynton Manor Farm
High Ercall
Sugdon
Marsh Green
0 kilometres 1
0 miles ½
Isombridge Farm

then follow its driveway to a road. Follow it right past Pool House Farm and a side road. Continue along the road enjoying a good leg stretch through the scattered settlement of Muckleton to eventually reach a junction by Muckleton Hall Farm.

2 Turn right on the signposted SW along a track past farm buildings, then continue with the hedge-lined track to its end. Go through the waymarked gate ahead and follow the signposted wide path ahead across the large field, shortly angling right to a stile. Go ahead across the very large crop field – *watered by a gigantic moveable machine* – then from midway continue along a green track

53

Poynton Manor Farm

Turn left along the road to Poynton Manor Farm. *Its timber-framed house dates from the 16thC, but integrated into a farm building by the road is part of a former 15thC chapel.* Here cross a stile on the left to a small gate beyond. Go across the field to a large footbridge over the river and up through trees. Continue ahead along the right-hand edge of a large field to a track, then across the next field. In its corner turn right along a hedge/tree lined green track, then left along a road into High Ercall. *The village, dating from Saxon times, developed around St Michael's church founded in the late 11thC and the adjoining 13thC fortified manor house, which was a Royalist stronghold during the Civil War, eventually falling to Parliamentary forces in 1646.*

2 At the main road go along Church Road opposite. At its end by the church turn right along a signposted enclosed path past houses to a road. Go through the gate opposite and follow the path along the long field edge to a stile. Go along the next field edge to a gate, past sewerage works then angle slightly left to a stile/gate. Turn right across the cattle grid and along an access lane towards Lower Grounds Farm. Before another cattle grid turn left through a gate into the right of two fields. Follow the tree boundary on your left along the field and through a gap in the corner. Turn right along the next field edge to a gate, then go along a green track. When it bends left continue past a large concrete area and along another track. When it bends right turn left between trees to a gate and follow the hedged/tree-lined path to a road junction at Sugdon. Go along the road opposite through the hamlet of Marsh Green. At the T-junction turn right to the bend of the road at Isombridge Farm.

SHREWSBURY TO WELLINGTON

13½ miles

24 The Square, Shrewsbury – B5062, near Haughmond Abbey

4½ miles

From the town centre the Shropshire Way heads to the English Bridge, then follows the meandering river Severn out of Shrewsbury. It is easy walking and includes a designated recreational route following the line of the disused Shrewsbury Canal, some sections still evident, to Uffington. It then continues through attractive woodland beneath Haughmond Hill.

The Shrewsbury Canal, largely forgotten, linked the town with a coalfield in an area now occupied by Telford, when it opened in 1797. Thomas Telford was involved in its construction and the 17 mile canal included several pioneering features: the Berwick Tunnel, the first to include a towpath, the cast iron trough used on the Longdon on Tern aqueduct and an incline plane at its eastern end linking with a higher canal serving the coalfield. It also used 6 ft wide horse-drawn tub boats, rather than narrowboats, to carry its cargo of coal.

In 1835 it finally became connected to the national canal network, with the opening of the new Newport Branch canal. By 1846 it was part of the Shropshire Union system. It was the main transport corridor for Shrewsbury, trading in iron ore, limestone, building materials, dairy products and other goods. Increasing competition from the railways led to its gradual decline. The Shrewsbury basin (now the railway station car park) was closed in 1922 and all remaining trade had ceased by the late 1930s and in 1944 the canal was abandoned. The Shrewsbury & Newport Canals Trust is working to protect and ultimately restore a navigable waterway.

From the statue of Clive cross to the Halifax/Santander banks opposite and turn right along the one-way

55

High Street to St Julian's Centre, then go along Wyle Cop. Cross Dogpole – *with the 17thC Lion Hotel opposite, a famous coaching inn on the London-Holyhead route –* and continue down Wyle Cop to the English Bridge. Descend steps then turn left along the cycle/walkway beside the river Severn. Follow it under the railway bridge then pedestrian bridge to its end at the weir. Go past seats and along the adjoining road, soon on the wide verge. At the bend of the road go through a small gate and follow a path beside the river, shortly passing under a road bridge. Later it leaves the tree-lined river, passes through trees, crosses a stream, and bends left up to a junction of cycle/walkways.

2 Turn right signposted to Uffington and follow the recreational route along the former towpath of the disused Shrewsbury Canal and past a turning to Sports Village, then continue along the wide bridleway, over a road, and on past Pimley Manor and under the A49. Continue along the embanked tree-lined bridleway, then go through a kissing gate on the right. Follow the path across open ground to another kissing gate, then down through trees, past a house – *with a view of the nearby river –* then up Mill Lane to the road in Uffington. Turn right past Holy Trinity church then at The Corbert Arms cross the road and go along the driveway opposite to a stile/gate by houses. Follow a green track to cross a bridge over the old canal. Go across the field to a small gate/stile and along a path through trees. Turn right along a wide path

under a nearby pylon and on along the edge of the wood. At a waymarked path junction, bend left and follow the path through The Hollies, attractive Forestry Commission woodland – *passing hidden Haughmond quarry, which has produced red sandstone for centuries, used to build Shrewsbury Castle and Abbey –* to the B5062, opposite Abbey Wood car park and the nearby driveway to Haughmond Abbey, which is well worth a visit.

25 B5062, near Haughmond Abbey to Isombridge Farm
5½ miles

This section takes you through Haughmond Hill woodland site, with its café.and popular forest trails, to a great viewpoint. It then heads east across farmland, passing through Roddington village, enjoying regular views of The Wrekin.

I Turn right up the roadside verge, then right along a side road signposted to Upton Magna. Follow it past Haughmond Quarry entrance, then turn right along a road leading to Haughmond Hill Forestry Commission site. Take its left fork and when it bends right into the main car park follow the wide stony track ahead to an information board on various forest trails. *Nearby is a café with toilets.* At a finger post beyond follow the signposted 'Walking Trails' wide path through the mixed woodland. At a junction of paths continue ahead on the right fork (red/blue) through a more open area, soon narrowing

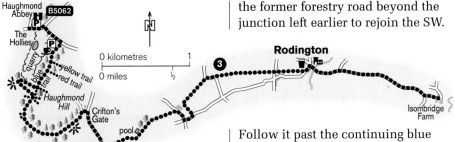

the former forestry road beyond the junction left earlier to rejoin the SW.

then bending left to where the trails split. Keep ahead on the blue trail to a T-junction with a former forestry road. The current shown SW route turns left, but my preferred route is to turn right, continuing with the blue trail to a toposcope at a superb viewpoint looking west to Shrewsbury and beyond.

Haughmond Hill comprises some of the oldest rocks in Shropshire. Nearby is the site of a small univallate late Bronze Age hillfort. It contains the remains of a late 18thC two-storey folly known as Haugmond Castle, used to signal local foxhunts, as well as a mortar emplacement said to have been used for Home Guard training during World War II. On a lower knoll lower is the remains of a ringwork, known as Queen Eleanor's Bower, a rare fortification built during the late Anglo-Saxon–late 12thC period. Nearby is a place known as Douglas's Leap, where the Earl of Douglas reputedly fell from his horse whilst attempting to escape from Henry IV's army after the Battle of Shrewsbury in 1403.

Continue along the waymarked narrow blue trail through trees to join

Follow it past the continuing blue trail on the right, and when it bends half-left angle right along a path down through trees to a path junction. Turn right along the returning blue trail, then at a waymark post turn left down a narrow stony public path through trees. Where waymarked Walk 5 angles back on the right, follow the path ahead past nearby Downton Hall then along the wood edge to eventually reach a forestry road at Criftin's Gate. Follow it right down to a road. Turn right along the road past The Hollow.

2 Shortly, with the 30 mph sign at Upton Magna in sight, turn left along a green track. Follow it along the large field edge and through a gap in the corner, then turn right across a sleeper bridge. Just beyond bear left across the field to the right-hand embanked corner of a large hidden pool. Continue on a green track along the field edge to a stony track. Turn left, then right along the field/wood edge to a waymarked gap. Go slightly right across the next large field to a road by Hunkington Farm. Follow it right, then at crossroads turn left. Shortly turn left on the waymarked Shropshire Way through a hedge gap and go along the large field. Midway angle across the field to a footbridge in its right-hand corner. Follow the bridleway through trees, then go along the road ahead.

3 On the bend cross a stile ahead and go through several fields to another road. Follow a path opposite across a large field to the road in Roddington. Turn left through the village. *Roddington is an ancient Saxon agricultural settlement lying by the river Roden, with a church dating from the 11thC. After 1797 it became an important haulage point on the Shrewsbury Canal, with its own wharves. Sadly nothing now remains of the splendid aqueduct that crossed the river.* At a crossroads near the Bull's Head turn right. After crossing the river the road passes Roddington Hall. Shortly take a narrow road on the right signposted to Isombridge. At a junction bend let to reach Isombridge Farm on the bend.

26 Isombridge Farm to Bowring Park, Wellington
3½ miles

The trail continues briefly by the attractive river Tern to Allscott, crosses farmland to the historic village of Wrockwardine, then heads to the historic market town of Wellington.

I From the bend take the signposted bridleway along a stony track past outbuildings. When it bends right bear left to a gate and another ahead. The bridleway follows the attractive river Tern south to cross a large footbridge over it, then passes former Allscott

Mill and follows its access track to the road. Follow it right through Allscott to the Plough Inn on the B4394 at Cross Green. The waymarked route goes across a field opposite, then over the railway line. (The next section may be hindered by potato crops.) After continuing south across a field for about 300 yards it turns north east back across the field, then along a track past Hollandstile back to the B4394. Turn right to a nearby gate. Follow a stiled path up two fields, then go up the road. At the junction keep ahead through the attractive village of Wrockwardine. *Standing on high ground between the north Shropshire Plain and The Wrekin, this ancient settlement developed around St Peter's church, of Saxon origin. The village was just north of Watling Street, the ancient trackway and Roman road, which became a major highway from the Middles Ages.* At the junction by the church turn left down the road's right-hand side then turn right past the side of the village hall to the end of its car park. Follow a path across the field to a stile, then up the next field edge to a road. Follow it left.

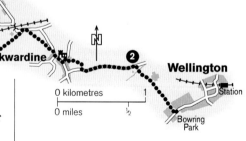

2 Later, just before power cables, turn right along a driveway, then just before the house left along an

enclosed path to a kissing gate. Turn right down the rough field edge to a footbridge over a stream into another field. Pass to the left of a telegraph pole and continue to the waymarked right-hand corner of the small wood ahead. Go through a wide hedge gap to a stile and a kissing gate beyond. Follow the path by a large fence, shortly angling away to join another path. Follow it left to a kissing gate. Turn left along the road through an estate in Wellington. At its end turn right up a signed enclosed path between dwellings, then left between hedges. Go past garages and on to the end of West Road. Go along the stony road ahead to a main road. Turn left along the pavement opposite to the entrance to Bowring Park.

WELLINGTON TO IRONBRIDGE

10½ miles

A fascinating section of contrasts featuring two of the Shropshire Way's highlights, one shaped by nature and the other by man. First The Wrekin, a small wooded hill (1335 ft/407 metres) containing an ancient hillfort and offering panoramic all-round views, then Ironbridge Gorge World Heritage Site, with its many museums. Although short in distance there is much to see and enjoy.

Wellington is an ancient settlement said to be named after an Anglo Saxon farmer. It lies near Watling Street, one of the country's most important Roman Roads. After it was granted a Market Charter in 1244, it grew into an important market town. In the early 19thC it was an important stop on the London to Holyhead coaching road. It prospered with the development of the iron industry and coalmining, then by the opening of the Crewe to Shrewsbury railway and a branch line to Craven Arms in the mid

19thC. In 1879 there were iron and brass foundries, nail and agricultural implement makers, and an extensive malting business.

27 Bowring Park, Wellington to Little Wenlock

6½ miles

After leaving Wellington the trail climbs through The Ercall, an ancient oak woodland Nature Reserve, and descends to the valley. It then begins a long steady climb up a stony track to the summit of The Wrekin, before descending, sometimes steeply, through woodland and continuing to the attractive village of Little Wenlock.

The Wrekin is probably the best known hill in Shropshire, and the subject of many legends. Made largely of volcanic rock and standing at 1335 ft/407 metres it dominates the mid-county skyline between Shrewsbury

59

and Telford. Whilst not the highest hill in Shropshire, it offers breathtaking all-round views, said to cover 15 counties. Its summit is crowned with a 20 acre Iron Age hillfort built around 400 BC and home to the Carnovii tribe until the Roman period. The Wrekin later became part of a Royal Forest. The Wrekin has been a popular place to visit for centuries and has hosted summer fairs. Interestingly the hill features in an often spoken local expression 'all round the Wrekin' meaning 'the long way round'.

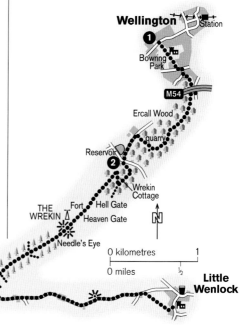

1 Go along a nearby enclosed surfaced path adjoining the park and follow it to a road. Cross to the pavement opposite and turn left, then right along Ercall Lane. Turn left along nearby Christine Avenue then turn right along an enclosed signposted path between houses and on up through a wood. When the path splits turn left to cross a large footbridge over a stream and continue to a road. Follow it right under the motorway bridge, then turn right on a signposted path back into the wood to cross a footbridge over the stream. (The next section through Ercall Wood is shared with Wrekin Forest waymarked coloured trails.) Follow the path south, soon rising. At a path junction, continue ahead, rising gently through the wood, past side paths, then on a long steady climb with the red/green trails. At a path T-junction turn left and follow the wide path down through the mature woodland. At a path junction keep ahead down the waymarked stony path past an information board at the site

of a former quarry – *which provided stone for the nearby A5.* Just past a small pool, where the red/green trails do a U-turn left, follow the waymarked SW/yellow trail down to a road. Follow it left down past a reservoir.

2 At a road junction turn right to nearby gates on the left giving access to The Wrekin. Follow the initially wide stony track on a long steady meandering climb through woodland to level out at Wrekin Cottage. *Better known as Halfway House it was said to have been built as a hunting lodge, but for generations its owners have offered drinks and snacks to walkers, or at one time, people being carried on donkeys to the summit.* After a stile/gate continue ahead along the stony track, soon bending sharp left and rising steadily.

It briefly levels out then rises again to an information board on the Wrekin Hillfort at its lower entrance known as Hell Gate. The track continues up through the middle of the fort. When it splits keep ahead through the remains of inner ramparts, known as Heaven Gate – *the fort's main entrance, once protected with guardhouses.* Continue past the nearby tall transmitter mast to a trig point and circular toposcope. Continue south-west along the ridge past a rocky outcrop, containing a cleft known as the Needle's Eye, to begin a long steady descent, shortly more steeply through woodland containing roe deer, to a crossroad of stony paths. Continue down the one ahead through trees, soon rising onto Little Hill then bending left steeply down through conifers to a cross-track. Follow the wide path ahead down to another track then continue down the waymarked path ahead through the wood and on to a road. Follow it left – *enjoying a good view of The Wrekin.* Later you reach a second side road on the right by Leighton Meadow and Holly Cottage. About 60 yards further turn right along a track to gates, then go along the left-hand edge of two fields and up the next to a kissing gate by a seat. After a small gate follow the path up through trees, then a lane past houses to a junction opposite St Lawrence's church in Little Wenlock. *Little Wenlock is one of the highest villages in Shropshire. The settlement's links to pre-historic times was confirmed by a hoard of broken Bronze Age spears found nearby in 1835 by a labourer cutting a drain. It is said to have been part of the Much Wenlock*

Priory estate, so hence its name. From the 17thC there began increasing exploitation of the area's mineral wealth, with open cast coal mining in particular playing an important part in the village's economy and contributing to the industrial revolution in Coalbrookedale. St Lawrence's church dating from the 12thC, contains a 1611 dated cast iron grave slab and other interesting old items.

28 Little Wenlock to Ironbridge
4 miles

This section crosses farmland then makes a dramatic descent into Coalbrookdale via Lydebrook Dingle, and an old tramway above Loamhole gorge. It then continues down to the Museum of Iron in the heart of the historic industrial community. After a short climb to the Rotundra viewpoint on Lincoln Hill, it descends to Ironbridge and the world famous cast iron bridge over the river Severn which gave the town its name.

I Turn right along Church Lane and at the junction go ahead along Buildwas Lane – *an ancient highway to Much Wenlock.* Later, when the now stony track splits just before the gated entrance to a large house ahead, cross a stile on the left. Follow the green track along the field edge and on to a stile between transmitter masts. Go along the large field edge. Midway angle left across the field to a gateway onto The Moors farm's access track. Follow it down to Coalbrookdale Road. Follow it right across a high bridge over the

A4169, then immediately turn left along a driveway past a bungalow. Just before Leasows Farm turn right to a large black iron gate, then go down the field to a stile into Lydebrook Dingle. Follow the waymarked path down the impressive ancient wooded gorge, then continue with the Rope Walk along a track – *a former 17thC horse-drawn tramway used to move limestone and sandstone to Coalbrookdale furnaces – above the deep wooded Loamhole valley. It then passes through a traditional unimproved hay meadow, and continues by the walled boundary of the former Sunnyside Estate deer park to Darby Road. Opposite is the signposted old Quaker burial ground.* Go down the road past grand houses to the old railway viaduct built in 1864 across Upper Furnace Pool – *which served a large waterwheel that powered machinery in the nearby furnace.*

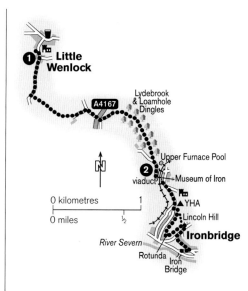

2 Turn right along the road beneath the viaduct then left under it along Coach Road past the Museum of Iron. *The museum contains one of the world's most important industrial monuments – the blast furnace that Abraham Darby succeeded in 1709 in using coke, instead of charcoal, made from coal to smelt iron. Until then charcoal made from timber produced only small amounts of iron. This breakthrough led to the mass-production of good quality cast iron, and turned the tiny hamlet of Coalbrookdale into a thriving industrial community at the cutting edge of the Industrial Revolution. The area was rich in raw materials used in*

iron-making: iron ore, coal deposits near the surface, sand, clay and limestone, water for power and a river for transport.

During the 18th and 19th centuries the Coalbrookdale ironworks run by successive generations of Darby's family produced a vast range of iron products, including rails, steam cylinders, fireplaces, gates and many. decorative items. By the mid 19thC it was the largest ironworks in the world, employing up to 4,000 men. The iron trade then gradually diminished in face of competition from elsewhere, but the tradition continues today with castings for the famous Aga/Rayburn cookers.

The area also became home to other important British industries, including the making of clay tobacco pipes, decorative ceramic tiles used in public buildings, including tube stations and the Houses of Parliament and still produced by hand using

Victorian methods, and the famous Coalport China porcelain. During the 20thC industrial activity steadily declined, leaving many remains of the area's industrial heyday. Ironbridge Gorge's importance was recognised in 1986 by its designation as a UNESCO World Heritage Site, which contains ten fascinating museums to visit.
Continue past nearby Enginuity and up to a junction. Go along the pavement past nearby Church Road, then Coalbrookdale Foundry. Continue along the opposite side of the road, then go along Paradise road beneath the large mid-19thC youth hostel. Shortly the waymarked SW turns left up a rough lane between houses. Midway turn right and follow a signposted path, soon stepped, up wooded Lincoln Hill. At a crossroad of paths go down the right fork signposted to Ironbridge, then take the left fork signposted 'Rotundra' along the wood edge past a viewpoint over rooftops to the power station. Shortly turn left up a stepped path to an information board on the site of a rotunda – *built in the late 18thC by Quaker Ironmaster Richard Reynolds, as a feature of local Sunday walks he created for his workers. Visible is the famous arched Iron Bridge in the deep wooded valley, its western end dominated by the cooling towers of the 1960's Ironbridge power station. To help them blend in with the landscape red pigment was added to the concrete* *to reflect the colour of the soil.*
Continue along the wide path across the wooded top of Lincoln Hill. At a path junction turn right signposted to Lincoln Hill Road, then left along an access track to the nearby road. Turn right down the road past Hodgebower Road then go down Church Hill to a roundabout in Ironbridge. Turn right along High Street past The Square to the famous bridge.
Lying in a beautiful wooded gorge, the stunning first iron bridge in the world remains a potent symbol of the Industrial Revolution. With the expansion of industrial activity the need for a bridge over the river to link Coalbrookdale with Broseley became ever greater. As the river was the main route used to transport raw materials and goods the bridge needed to be single arched to accommodate passing boats. It was built by Abraham Darby III, the grandson of the original ironmaster, based on a design by architect Thomas Pritchard, as an innovative way of showing the versatility of cast iron. It was opened on New Year's Day 1781. The bridge, made of five arches, stands 55 feet high above the river. 378 tons of iron was used, with casting done at local foundries. Tolls were charged, although the tollhouse was not built until 1783. It now houses an interesting exhibition on the bridge. Afterwards a separate town developed beside the bridge.

IRONBRIDGE TO WILDERHOPE MANOR
12 miles

29 Ironbridge to Much Wenlock
4½ miles

This section passes through attractive Benthall Edge Wood, once exploited for its coal, clay, limestone and sandstone, but now a haven for wildlife, and offering delightful woodland trails. It offers the opportunity to divert to visit nearby National Trust owned 16thC Benthall Hall (*check opening times*).
It continues across farmland to enter the historic small town of Much Wenlock along a delightful section of old railway line.

I Cross the Iron Bridge and go past the Toll House. At an information board on Benthall Edge Woodland bear right, then follow the nearby waymarked Severn Valley Way and coloured trails along the former Kidderminster–Shrewsbury railway line (1872-1960) passing under a bridge and continuing to an information board on nearby Bower Yard lime kiln – *which produced quicklime for agriculture and building from the mid 19thC until the 1940s.* A little further along the railway track turn left to a finger post, then right, signposted 'Cooling Tower by ridge path'. The wide path rises beside the fence above the railway track and continues along the bottom edge of the

wood, then descends to a kissing gate at a crossroad of paths. Bear left up the sunken path signposted to Benthall Hall, then take its waymarked left fork to a kissing gate. After a long steady climb through the wood the path eventually levels out at a small gate, by the bridleway leading to Benthall Hall. Follow the wide path ahead along the wooded top of Benthall Edge. At a waymarked path/bridleway junction, follow the narrow path ahead, soon along the top wood edge, to a stile into a field. Go along its edge, then down the next field to Cowslip Cottage. Follow its access track to a road at Wyke. Follow it right past a side road and Manor Farm and on past Audience Wood. *When it bends left a gate on the right offers a view of nearby Tickwood Hall, an early 19thC manor house and the former home of Lady Katherine Dugdale, who served the Queen as a Lady-in Waiting for almost 50 years, until 2002.* Shortly the road descends.

2 In the dip turn sharp left on the signposted path along a track through the wood, soon rising and bending to Woodhouse Farm. Go along a green track ahead to a kissing gate, then along the field edge. At a waymarked gap in the boundary take the second path leading left up to a tree, where it bends right to a kissing gate. At a field beyond turn left along its edge to a kissing gate. Go along the edge of the next large field, then mid-way go half-right towards the middle of Bradley farm to a kissing gate. Go between outbuildings and past the house to a road. Go along a hedge-lined green track ahead, then along the edge of two fields to cross a large footbridge over a stream. Follow the enclosed path past Downs Mill and go along its access track then up a road. When it bends left follow a waymarked path ahead up through trees and down onto the former Buildwas-Much Wenlock railway line (1862-1964).

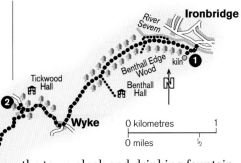

Turn left along the delightful section of tree-lined railway cutting, now Much Wenlock Railway Walk, to an information board on its history. Just beyond bend right to a gate. *Ahead on Linden Field, previously named Windmill Field, after the old windmill overlooking it, is a sculpture to Dr. William Penny-Brookes 1809-95. It was here that the first Wenlock Games he organised were held in 1850.* Turn left then continue ahead along the road past the nearby former Much Wenlock railway station. Just beyond turn left along a stony path, soon enclosed, to a road by the nearby priory , which you may wish to visit. Turn right past Priory Hall, formerly the National School 1848-1952, along a road known as the Bull Ring – *where bull-baiting was popular until the early 19thC –* past early 17th C cottages. Turn left past 12thC Holy Trinity Church and the 16thC timber-framed Guildhall to

the town clock and drinking fountain – *commemorating Queen Victoria's Diamond Jubilee –* in The Square, opposite the Memorial Hall Museum and Visitor Information Centre.

There is evidence of pre-historic man in the area and of Roman occupation in the 1st Century AD, but a first settlement here was a double monastery for both nuns and monks, with separate churches, founded about 680 by King Merewalh of Mercia. His daughter Milburge became the abbess and was later proclaimed a saint, because of her said miracles. In the 11thC a new minster was built on the site by the Earl of Mercia, then the Normans established a priory of Cluniac monks, which prospered until Henry VIII's Dissolution of the Monasteries in 1540.

During the 12thC a settlement began to grow near the priory, and in 1224 it received a charter to hold weekly markets. It lay at an intersection of important trading routes, especially the medieval road from Shrewsbury to London. It.later became an important staging post where coach horses were changed after a steep climb up Wenlock Edge.

The small town prospered and was granted a Borough charter in 1468,

65

but it remained under the control and influence of the priory until its dissolution.

Among the town's trades at various times were the making of cloth, shoes, needles, tobacco pipes, paper, as well as tanning and malting. But the town became best known for the limestone it quarried from Wenlock Edge for use as building stone and lime. From the early 18thC until the late 19thC its limestone was in great demand as flux for iron smelting in Coalbrookdale, and in 1862 a railway was opened to improve its transport. Limestone quarrying for the construction industry continued throughout the 20thC but has recently finished.

Much Wenlock played a key role in inspiring the International Olympic Games. In 1850, William Penny Brookes, a local doctor and JP, established the Wenlock Olympian Class (later renamed Olympian Society). The popular Wenlock Olympic Games were held each Whit Tuesday on Linden Field, watched by about 8,000 people, with prizes not only for physical activities, but for proficiency in arts and sciences. In 1865 he was a founder of the National Olympic Association, but his long term dream was for an International Olympic Games in Athens. Sadly he died just four months before the first one was held in 1896. Wenlock Olympian Games are still held each year.

30 Much Wenlock to Wilderhope Manor
7½ miles

This section goes along the famous wooded Wenlock Edge, one of the most notable natural features in Shropshire, to the National Trust owned Elizabethan Manor House, now a youth hostel. Changes have been made to the original route to maximise the pleasure of walking along this limestone ridge. It later utilises a section of the former single track Wellington – Craven Arms railway.

Wenlock Edge is a Silurian limestone escarpment, stretching for over 18 miles from Much Wenlock to Craven Arms. It was formed as a coral reef south of the Equator millions of years ago under a shallow tropical sea. The fossil-rich limestone is one of Britain's most important geological sites and a Site of Special Scientific Interest. The woodland that covers its top and steep northern slopes is an important habitat for wildlife and many plants, some rare. It has featured in music by Vaughan Williams, in poetry by A E Houseman, in a novel by Mary Webb and in works of art by L S Lowry. Parts of the Edge are owned by the National Trust and it now a popular recreational area for walkers and horseriders, with plans for cycling trails.

Wilderhope Manor

The limestone has been quarried since the Middle Ages for use in many local buildings, including Much Wenlock Priory, and for creating *lime for use as a fertiliser. From the beginning of the 18thC quarries developed along Wenlock Edge to meet the demand for limestone used for fluxing in iron-making production at Coalbrookedale during the Industrial Revolution. Later the limestone was used for road stone and hard core, and making cement. As late as 1979 about 100 people still worked in the quarries.*

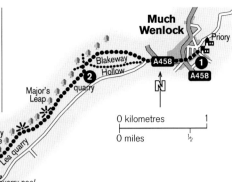

I Go along the right-hand side of the High Street past the library and timber-framed Raynalds Mansion – *whose 17thC frontage conceals a medieval hall.* At the junction with the A548 cross Smithfield Road opposite the Gaskell Arms Hotel – *a 17thC coaching inn* – and continue along the pavement beside the A548 past the B4378. After a railed raised section of pavement cross to the opposite side then turn left along the B4371. After about 150 yards turn right across the road, signposted to Blakeway Hollow – *an old packhorse route over Wenlock Edge to Shrewsbury* – to go up a road opposite. Soon the signposted Shropshire Way turns right and follows a path up through trees to a kissing gate, then up through the edge of woodland, soon taking its left fork,

to go through a waymarked gate at its corner. Go along a path, then take its right fork up across open ground, past an old quarry and on to a gate in the field's right-hand corner. Turn left to a kissing gate then right along the next field edge to a small gate by Stokes Barn. Go through a car parking area for the Edge Adventure Activities Centre and through a gate, then follow the stony track to a stile/gate. Continue ahead across the field then go through the left of facing gates. Go along the next field edge to a kissing gate to join the tree-lined bridleway beyond (Blakeway Hollow). Follow it past another bridleway to a waymarked bridleway junction by a National Trust Wenlock Edge sign. Turn left on the waymarked Shropshire Way to pass between barriers.

2 Follow the path along the wood/field edge – *with a view ahead of Brown Clee Hill* – then along the wooded top of Wenlock Edge past a former large quarry, then the signposted 'Major's Leap' viewpoint. *It takes its name from the spot where Major Thomas Smallman of Wilderhope Manor, a Royalist officer* *who whilst trying to evade capture from pursuing Roundheads made his horse jump off the edge. While Smallman survived, his mount died and his ghost still haunts there.* Continue along the main path between the vast former quarry 'canyon' and the steep wooded slope of Blakeway Coppice, passing another viewpoint towards The Wrexin, then two bridleways. *Lea quarry, with a water-fillled workings near its end, was the last to close in 2010. Edge Renewables now use it to process timber into wood chip biomass fuel pellet, whilst undertaking a project to landscape the site to encourage wildlife and plants and to create a visitor centre.* At the end of the quarry the path splits at a waymark post. Turn left down through trees to a cross-path by the top of limekilns. Turn right past a bird hide and on through trees to an information board at Knowle Quarry face. The path rises and continues through trees to join another waymarked path which takes you to Wenlock Edge car park. Turn right along the road, then take the nearby road signposted to Hughley angling down through Wenlock Edge.

3 At the access track leading to Lower Hill Farm turn left up a signposted sunken path through trees to a small gate. Turn right along a level green track. *This is the former railway line, built in stages during the 1860's, which connected Wellington to the Shrewsbury–Hereford line just north of Craven Arms. In 1951 passenger services on this section from Much*

Wenlock ended and the complete branch line closed in 1963, a year after the last train ran. Follow the old railway along the lower wooded slope of Wenlock Edge, crossing two minor roads, then after 2½ miles you reach a sign saying 'No public access from this point'. Here turn left and follow the waymarked Shropshire Way bridleway up across the wooded slope, over a road and up through trees, soon levelling out and meeting a sunken stony track. Turn left up it, soon bending left, to a road. Do a U-turn right and follow the gated bridleway along the top of wooded Wenlock Edge, the edge of two fields, then a wood to a waymarked bridleway/path junction. Continue along the next field edge and through a wide gap in the corner. Here the Shropshire Way leaves the bridleway and the Wenlock Edge, and turns left along the edge of two fields down to the small car park and stony track at Wilderhope Manor and nearby farm.

Wilderhope Manor is a grand Grade 1 listed Elizabethan gabled manor house, dating from 1585. It was built for Francis Smallman and remained in the family until the estate was sold in 1734. It steadily fell into disuse and in 1936 it was bought by the W A Cadbury Trust, who then donated it to the National Trust for restoration and use as a youth hostel, which continues to this day. Many of the original features survive. It has a history of ghostly sightings, including that of a small child and one of a tabby cat. Sleep well!

WILDERHOPE MANOR TO CRAVEN ARMS 10½ miles OR CHURCH STRETTON 11½ miles

From Wilderhope Manor, rather than continuing south over the Clee Hills, then west to Ludlow, you now have two alternative shorter route options to either Craven Arms or Church Stretton, utilsing new waymarked sections of the Shropshire Way.

31 Wilderhope Manor to Wolverton Wood
6 miles

This section of easy walking continues south westwards beside or through wooded Wenlock Edge, later passing through Harton Hollow Nature Reserve, to Wolverton Wood, where the trail splits.

1 Go up Wilderhope Manor's stony access track, then follow its driveway to a road. Take the signposted bridleway through the field opposite, then along Wenlock Edge through Coats Wood and later Roman Bank, both owned by the National Trust. Continue along a houses's stony access track to a road junction. Go along the road ahead past a car parking area, then turn right and follow a bridleway along Marked Ash's access track past a house, then up past another. The bridleway continues along the steep wooded slope of Wenlock Edge into a field. Continue along the right-hand field edge besides Stars Coppice.

2 At its corner by an incoming bridleway continue ahead, soon along the field/wood edge to a small gate. Follow the waymarked gated path along the edge of several more fields and through a narrow strip of woodland.

Go briefly along the next field edge, through a gate just before its corner, then continue through mature woodland along Wenlock Edge to eventually reach a road. Go up the bridleway opposite through woodland – *part of Harton Hollow Nature Reserve* – then along its edge to a small car park. Turn right along the road past a track then turn left up a path through trees then follow the waymarked bridleway along wooded Wenlock Edge to a signposted junction of Shropshire Way routes at Wolverton Wood.

69

32 Wolverton Wood to The Discovery Centre, Craven Arms

4½ miles

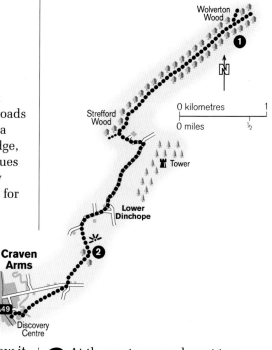

This section continues with the bridleway along wooded Wenlock Edge, then follows quiet country roads to beyond Lower Dinchope. After a short climb onto a small grassy ridge, offering extensive views, it continues through fields to the small railway town of Craven Arms (see page 85 for details).

1 Continue ahead, signposted to Craven Arms, with the wide bridleway along the top edge of the wooded slope for nearly 1¾ miles. After emerging from trees the bridleway turns left down a hedge-lined track to a road. Follow it down and up to a staggered junction. Go up the road ahead, soon bending right. *Visible on nearby Callow Hill above woodland is Flounders' Folly, a lookout tower built in 1838 by Benjamin Flounders, a prominent Quaker and entrepreneur.* The road descends steadily then continues to a junction by Folly View at Lower Dinchope. Turn right past nearby Lower Dinchope Farm and down past a side road. At a junction go up the road ahead. then at its brow cross a stile on the left. Follow a faint green track up the hillside and continue to a visible waymark post, then go along the wide grassy ridge past a seat.

2 At the next waymark post turn right down to a stile. Descend the wooded slope, then follow a stiled path down through two fields and along the edge of another to a road. Cross a stile opposite. Just beyond bear right along the edge of a long field to a stile. Go straight ahead across the next large field to a finger post at the far tree boundary. Cross a footbridge over the river and follow a narrow lane into Craven Arms. At a junction go along a rough lane ahead, then an initially enclosed path to a finger post marking a junction of Shropshire Way routes. Follow a path right to the Discovery Centre.

33 Wolverton Wood to The Square, Church Stretton

5½ miles

This section descends Wenlock Edge and heads northwards to Acton Scott Heritage Farm, then makes a short steep climb onto Ragleth Hill (1306 ft/398 metres), offering superb all-round views, before continuing into the attractive market town of Church Stretton below.

1 Take the path signposted to Acton Scott/ Church Stretton on a long steady descent through the trees to emerge into a large field. Turn left down a green track. Just before it bends right angle left along a wide path to cross a footbridge over a river. Go across the large field to a fence corner about 50 yards to the right of a large barn and round to a kissing gate onto a road. Go through a small gate opposite and follow the path angling left across a field to another. Turn right along a farm track below. At its end enter the right of two fields ahead. Follow the path through the large field and past a tree just before a waymarked path junction at the far side. Continue through trees, then angle left through the middle of the large reedy field, soon on a good path, passing two waymark posts. When the path continues by a line of trees angle right past two further posts to a stile 40 yards above the right-hand field corner. Angle right across the next field to a stile/gate at the wood corner. Go up the left-hand field edge to a stile. Just beyond the path bends

right up the edge of a small wood to a stile into a field. Go past the telegraph pole and across the corner of the field – *containing the site of a Roman villa –* to a stile/gate. *Nearby is the entrance to Acton Scott historic working farm, which is best known as the setting for BBC2's 'Victorian Farm' series.* Angle right to the road by Wenlock Lodge. Follow it left. At crossroads turn right towards Ragdon. At the entrance to Toad Hall the road bends right.

2 Soon cross a stile in the hedge/tree boundary on the left. Go up the field to a stile and down the next field to another. Go up through bracken to a stile onto Ragleth Hill. Follow the path up the steep hillside past a fence corner to a post/pole on its summit then follow a delightful wide path north-eastwards along the bracken-covered ridge. At the far end descend briefly towards Church Stretton, then turn right down to a nearby waymark post. Follow a path down through bracken then at a kissing gate by a welcome board turn left. Follow a path through bracken and down through

71

woodland by a fence, past side paths, to a stile. Continue to another stile, then along an enclosed path, soon bending down between bungalows. Go down the estate road (Poplar Drive). At the junction turn left down the road. At the next junction keep ahead, then just past Donkey Patch turn left down an enclosed path to another road. Angle left to go along another short enclosed path, then cross with care the A49. Go along the path opposite, over the Mynd Industrial Estate road and on to cross a large footbridge over the railway. Follow the enclosed surfaced path over two roads to the High Street by the King's Arms. Turn right along the pavement opposite to reach The Square. (For information on Church Stretton see pages 91/92)

View from Ragleth Hill

WILDERHOPE MANOR TO COLDGREEN
11¼ miles

The Shropshire Way follows the original route south from Wenlock Edge, but now includes a delightful loop to the summit of Abdon Burf, the highest point in Shropshire, and the first of Brown Clee Hill's twin peaks, before continuing to its second peak of Clee Burf. This hill section across moorland is exposed so be prepared for changeable weather conditions. The only public transport now from Coldgreen is R&B Travel's 141 school bus from the Three Horseshoes Inn on the B4364 to Ludlow at 16.00.

34 Wilderhope Manor to Bank House
5½ miles

This section heads south from Wenlock Edge across the eastern end of Corverdale, a wide attractive valley that once echoed to the sound of an iron industry, to historic Holdgate village. The route then continues across farmland to the base of Brown Clee Hill.

At a finger post cross a stile by a gate and turn right signposted to Brown Clee. Go along the field edge past Wilderhope farm buildings, then along a green track past the house into another field. When the track bends

left continue ahead down a greener track. When it bends half-right follow a path ahead, soon alongside the tree boundary, to a footbridge in the corner. Go along the next field's left-hand edge to a facing stile. Turn left through trees, over a footbridge and stile, then right along the field edge onto a farm track. Turn right then left over a nearby stile into a field. Follow the tree boundary round to cross a stile in it and continue to a stream and a stile. Turn right along **Holdgate** the field edge, then continue

through the next two fields, the second long, onto a nearby house's access track. Turn right across the stream then go half-left up the field to a road. Follow it left to a junction. Cross to the verge opposite and turn right, then left over a stile.

2 Go down the field edge, then bend right above the river Corve to cross a large gated footbridge. Follow the waymarked path along the edge of two

73

fields, then left to a gate onto a road. Cross a stile opposite and go along the field edge to cross two footbridges. Go along the long field edge, then up the next field to the road in Holdgate. *During the Doomsday Survey in 1086 the settlement contained a church and motte and bailey castle. It was held by Helgot, and subsequently took his name. Holdgate developed under various ownership into a much larger village than exists today, peaking in the early 19thC. The current Holy Trinity Church dates from the 12thC with later additions. In its porch a notice says 'Help yourself to refreshments inside the church, be it coffee, biscuits, divine inspiration, or all three'. The castle was in use until 1645, when it was partly destroyed during the Civil War and abandoned. The motte still remains. Nearby Holdgate Hall has a large 13thC round tower integrated into its farmhouse.*

Turn right along the road past two houses, then just before Holdgate Farm cross a stile on the left. Go past the barn and down the field to a gate. Go across the next to a stile into another field. Continue ahead, soon between tree boundaries, to a stile. Go up the next field edge to a stile on the left opposite a small old house (Blue Hall) into the adjoining field. Turn right up its edge, then ahead across the field to a stile. Continue up the next field to a stile in the tree boundary. The path angles left up across the wooded slope to a stile. Turn left along the field edge and on to a gate. Turn right up the edge of two fields to a facing stile in the corner. Just beyond follow an enclosed

green track to nearby Earnstrey Hall, then its access track to a road.

3 Cross the stile opposite and go across the field to a stile/sleeper bridge/stile in the corner. Go across the next field to a stile in its right-hand corner. Turn left up the field edge to a gate, then go along the edge of the next two fields to a small gate. Turn left along the next field edge past New Earnstrey Park, then right up the road past Parkview. As it bends half-left cross a stile ahead. Descend between tree boundaries, cross two sleeper bridges, then turn right up the field edge above a sunken stream. Before the corner bend left to a stile in the far corner. Turn right up the road. At the junction turn left. At the next turn right (Cockshutford) by an Abdon noticeboard past 'The Little Red Bookshop' – *an old telephone box containing books for borrowing and exchanging by Abden residents.* Continue up the road to Bank House.

35 Bank House to the B4364, Coldgreen
5¾ miles

After a short climb up a sunken bridleway, the route goes around Abdon Burf's northern slopes, then follows a narrow road up to its summit (1771 ft/ 540 metres). It then descends to rejoin the bridleway and continues across moorland up to Abdon Burf (1673 ft / 510 metres). Later it makes a long steady descent with the attractive sunken tree-lined bridleway, then continues to the B4364.

Brown Clee Hill's twin peaks of Abdon Burf and Clee Burf have attracted man since pre-historic times. Abdon Burf was used for burials during the Bronze Age and both were once crowned by Iron Age hillforts, now largely destroyed by quarrying. Nordy Bank, to the west of Clee Burf, is the only surviving hillfort.

Brown Clee has been exploited for its mineral wealth since medieval times, when coal and iron ore were mined and used in a once thriving iron making works in nearby Coverdale. In later years until the late 1930s the hill was extensively quarried for dhustone (dolerite), a hard stone used in road surfacing. The hill carries the scars and relics of its industrial past, but all is now quiet, apart from work relating to its air traffic control radar masts.

On the bend just beyond Bank House and the entrance to Dingle Lodge go through a gate ahead. Follow the signposted bridleway up a narrow track, soon continuing up its right fork. At a waymarked small gate on the right turn left up to a waymark post. Continue across the mid-slopes of Abdon Burf below an old embanked boundary down to a gate. Follow the delightful waymarked green path ahead across the bracken-covered hillside. Just after a descending side path follow the left fork to a small gate, then continue beside a fence to a waymarked path junction at a wood corner. The delightful wide green path now follows the perimeter fence of the wood to a narrow road *– once an inclined tramway used to carry crushed stone from the quarries*

above. Turn right up the road, shortly bending past a former crushing house and other old structures, then a small water-filled quarry. Just before the wireless station and communication masts on Abdon Burf's summit turn left up to a toposcope for panoramic all-round views. Now follow the wide path down its western slope to a waymark post before old concrete fence posts, where you rejoin the bridleway.

2 Follow it left beside the fence across the heather moorland. At the fence corner follow the narrow green track/bridleway ahead through heather *– with the mast visible on Clee Burf –* down to a seat and gate. *Nearby is a small memorial stone to the 23 allied and German airmen who lost their lives in aircraft crashes on Brown Clee Hill during World War II.* Follow the path ahead, then take another angling left to join the boundary wall of a nearby wood. At its corner follow a path ahead near the wall on a long steady climb across the moorland, later circumventing a dense area of reeds by a wood then continuing by the boundary to

Bank House **1**

Abdon Burf

lake

2

memorial

Clee Burf

Coldgreen

B4364

0 kilometres 1

0 miles ½

75

a stile near the mast on Clee Burf. *Ahead is Titterstone Clee.* Follow the waymarked path to a fence corner, then left down through an area of old bell pits – *worked for coal until the end of the 19thC* – and on across the moorland to join the perimeter fence of a wood. At a gate the bridleway bends right beside the fence, then descends into a gully to a small gate. Continue down the narrow sunken bridleway

– *beware of holes* – to another gate, then down the wider bridleway past a house. The sunken tree-lined bridleway now makes a long steady descent, crosses a road and continues down to Newton Cottage. Go down its access track, then at a track junction by Fernbrook House turn left and follow the track on a long steady climb to Wheathill Lodge, then up its driveway to the B4364.

COLDGREEN TO LUDLOW 10 ¾ miles
OR CLEOBURY MORTIMER 10 miles

The trail continues across Titterstone Clee hill (1749 feet/533 metres), the third highest hill in Shropshire, then offers a choice of routes. The main one continues to Ludlow, whilst a new branch takes you to the small town of Cleobury Mortimer, near the southern-most tip of Shropshire, bordering Worcestershire. Please note that the weather on Titterstone Clee Hill is notoriously volatile at times, with winds and mist, when all below is calm and clear, so be prepared. The Diamond 2L Kidderminster-Ludlow bus connects with the route at Angel Bank, Clee Hill and Cleobury Mortimer.

36 B4364, Coldgreen to Titterstone Clee Hill quarry car park
3¾ miles

This section involves a climb onto Titterstone Clee Hill, reshaped by

extensive mining and quarrying, but offering great views.

Titterstone Clee Hill has been used by man since prehistoric times, with its top containing early burial mounds and the remains of a large Iron Age hillfort. But it was its rich mineral deposits that turned it into an important historic industrial landscape. From the medieval period it was mined for iron ore and coal from shallow bell pits, then from the mid 19thC extensively quarried for dhutstone. It became a major industrial area with hundreds of workers employed in the quarries. The stone was mainly used for pavement sets and for major engineering works, such as Cardiff Dock, then later for roadstone used in road building. Nowadays the hill is peaceful, but its vast disused quarries and many remaining structures, some early examples of the use of reinforced concrete, are a reminder of its important industrial past. On its top sits the large National Air Traffic Service radar dome, part of the system for monitoring UK airspace, and a Met Office weather station.

I Turn right then left up an enclosed track to Dodshill. At outbuildings cross a stile on the right. Angle left across the field to a small gate and a footbridge beyond. Go up the field to another small gate onto Knapp Farm's stony access track beyond. Follow it left to a road. Follow it right into Bromdon. On the bend turn right along a hedged track/bridleway, known as Callow lane. It passes a pool amongst trees, barns, and another small pool. When the track bends to a gate continue ahead along the delightful narrow tree-lined bridleway to a gate into the edge of moorland beneath Titterstone Clee. The waymarked bridleway continues ahead past nearby Callowgate. At a waymarked bridleway/path junction keep ahead on the path, rising steadily through a gap in bracken.

2 Shortly, at a crossroad of paths take the second on the left minor path angling through scattered bracken and reeds to a distinctive wide grassy slope leading up through the bracken towards the large globe-topped mast. Follow the good path up the slope. Just above the last area of bracken, take a clear path angling right up across the steep slope, then heading towards a dolerite scree slope beneath crags on Titterstone Clee's western end. Near the top just before a waymark post follow a good path along the rocky

edge to a trig point and small stone shelter for panoramic all-round views. *It is said that the hill derived its name from a giant rocking stone that was here.* Follow the path towards the nearest radar station, then the waymarked SW wide path along the edge of the vast quarry – *which closed in 1962 –* soon on a steady descent. *To your left is the vast East/ Radar quarry which opened in 1910.* Shortly, bend right down a narrow stony track and cross the bend of a road, with the large quarry car park nearby, to a post marking two branches of the Shropshire Way.

37 Titterstone Clee Hill quarry car park to the A4117, Angel Bank
1 ½ miles

This section descends through the quarry and the impressive Titterstone Incline, then follows a bridleway to Nine Springs Farm and across fields to Angel Bank. An alternative route to Clee Hill village from Nine Springs Farm is also described. The 2L bus to Ludlow can be caught from either Angel Bank or Clee Hill.

77

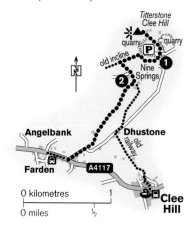

Take the waymarked SW angling right across the road and down into a hollow. Turn right along a former tramway through a stone-clad gap in the bank. Continue down a narrow stony track to the large concrete former crusher and sorter, then follow a path along the left edge of the large flat quarry working area, to a waymark post at the top of the Titterstone Incline – *down which quarried stone was transported by a cable-operated 3 foot narrow gauge railway, almost 2,000 yards long, from 1880-1954 to the Ludlow-Clee Hill railway (1864-1960) at Bitterley Wharf.* Descend the incline. Later, just after crossing a small bridge, turn left down the waymarked SW bridleway. Follow it across open ground, over a rough lane, down to a footbridge over a stream, up to a small gate, then up a field edge to a gate/stile by Nine Springs Farm. (For Clee Hill, go up to the house, then follow its access track to a road. Go down the road to Dhutstone. Turn left up a track between sections of Rouse Boughton Terrace then continue along a former railway line. At the outskirts of Clee

Hill turn right down a road, then left down The Crescent to the A4117 at Clee Hill. There is a bus stop by nearby Clee Hill Stores.)

2 For Angel Bank follow the SW bridleway right along the field edge to a bridle gate then across open ground by a line of telegraph poles to a gate. Continue through the edge of a rough field to a gate, then right along the next field edge to a small gate by a house. The waymarked bridleway angles half-left across the field to a gate and passes sheep pens to a gate at Sheep Farm. Go past the house to a gate ahead and angle left across the field to a gate in the corner. Go past Mountside's garden and along its access track to a road. Follow it right down to the A4117 at Angel Bank. (For the 2L bus to Ludlow turn right along the pavement down past Angel House. Cross to the large junction/turning for Knowbury, where the bus stops).

38 Titterstone Clee Hill quarry car park to Cleobury Mortimer
6¼ miles

This new waymarked branch heads eastwards across a moorland plateau, part of Clee Hill Common, then across farmland, passing through the attractive village of Hopton Wafers, to the small old market border town of Cleobury Mortimer. (From here it extends via Kinlet to link with the Severn Way long distance trail.)

Go down the road, then take a waymarked narrow old green track

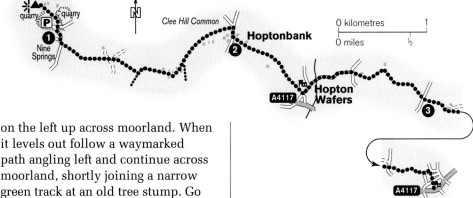

on the left up across moorland. When it levels out follow a waymarked path angling left and continue across moorland, shortly joining a narrow green track at an old tree stump. Go ahead briefly along it, then follow a path ahead to a waymark post. Cross a nearby farm's access track then follow a path ahead to the bend of another track. Continue ahead on a faint path across the reedy tussocky moorland, passing close to a small pool on the right, then turn right across its embanked end to a waymark post. Turn left along a good path to reach a stony track by old workings topped with small brick ruin. Follow it left to a house then down between two others. At the track junction turn right a few yards, then left down to another track. Turn left down it, then after passing between cottages, on the bend, keep ahead and follow the waymarked bridleway on a steady descent across the part reedy/gorse-covered Clee Hill Common to a house's hedge boundary corner. Continue down an old green track past another house, then turn left along Moral Cottage's access track, soon descending past side tracks. Just after it bends left towards a road, angle right across rough ground to the road junction. Turn right along the road through Hoptonbank.

2 Just after Wild Meadow boarding kennels, turn left along a stony access track past a bungalow, then a house. Pass to the left of another dwelling to a stile in the garden corner. Follow the waymarked stiled path through three fields, then down the next field to a footbridge in the left-hand corner. The waymarked route continues down through four further fields, passes through trees, crosses a stream, then turns left beside a field fence. After about 120 yards turn left down to a stile, over a stream, then bear right to two stiles. Continue to a kissing gate and through St. Michael and All Angel's churchyard to the road in Hopton Wafers. *The unusual second name refers to Robert de Walfre, who held the manor in the mid-13thC. The church was built in 1827 on the site of the original Norman church. Only the font remains from that time.* Follow it left past a side road, over the river, and up past the entrance to Hopton Court – *an 18thC house, with parkland, used for weddings and other functions –*

The Shropshire Way

and on to a T-junction. Go through a small gate opposite and over a stile. Go across the field to a small gate, through the garden past a house, over a stile at the end of a pool, and round to another stile. Go across two fields onto a track. Turn right to a nearby gate. Turn left along the field edge, then after about 70 yards, turn right across the field, soon by a hedge on your left, to go through a gate in it. Angle right down the field to a stream and a waymarked gate in the wooded boundary midway. Angle left up the next field to the small wood corner to cross a nearby stile. Follow a path through trees and up the large field to a road.

3 Take the nearby signposted stiled path through two fields. Continue beside the hedge, soon bending right to a small gate. Follow the waymarked path along two field edges round past a house to the stony access track. Follow the waymarked path across the nearby large field to a road. Go through the gate opposite and angle right across the field down to a stile below houses. Turn left along the surfaced path, soon going up its right fork through the park and bending right past the rugby pitch and floodlit sports area, then rising to a small gate. Go along the stony path, then behind the Sports & Social Club building to the bend of a road in Cleobury Mortimer. Go along the pavement ahead to crossroads by a primary school. Turn right along the road towards the church spire, then down a wide surfaced path, over Childe Road, and on down to the church.

Cleobury Mortimer, originally a Saxon settlement, became the main seat of the powerful Mortimer family, who were granted the manor in 1074, before moving to Ludlow, hence 'Mortimer' in its name. The settlement received its market charter in 1226. St Mary the Virgin church, with its famous twisted wooden spire, dates from 1160. It replaced an earlier one and stands near the site of the castle built by the Mortimers. After a period of decline the small town began to prosper again from the 16thC with the mining of iron ore. There were local furnaces and corn and paper mills powered by the river Rea. It supplied goods to the local agricultural and mining areas. In 1864 it had a station on the Bewdley–Tenbury branch railway, 2 miles away, then from 1908 one on the Cleobury Mortimer and Ditton Priors light railway. Both lines are now closed.

39 A4117, Angel Bank to Ludlow
5½ miles

This section follows field paths to an unusually low-lying atmospheric Iron Age hillfort (570 ft/174 metres), then continues on an attractive indirect route into the centre of the historic market town of Ludlow.

1 Go along a stony access track almost opposite. At the house turn right over a stile. Follow the path across the field to a stile by a house. Go along the hedged path past another house, then briefly down the hedged stony access track to cross a stile on the left. Go down to a stile/sleeper bridge/stile, then up to another stile. Go across the field, through a corner gap, then the next narrow field to a stile. Continue to another stile and one opposite, then

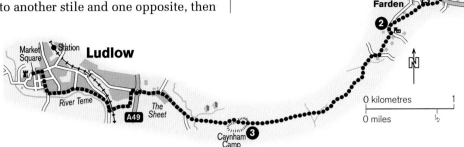

bear left to a stile and on past a shed to a gate and up to a stile. Follow a path angling right, soon contouring across the field's mid-slopes, then angle down to a stile/finger post by the road.

2 Follow the signposted path up the field and on beside the boundary round to a stile. Follow the narrow enclosed path down past the churchyard to a road. Cross a stile opposite and go along the field edge to a stile. Follow the narrow path beside the fence through two fields to a kissing gate, then the hedged/tree-lined path down to a road. Follow it right, then before the bend, turn left over a stile. Go down the field edge to another stile, then slightly right down the next field and through trees to a footbridge and stile beyond. Go across the next field and through the waymarked left of two gates. Continue down the field edge to go through a gate. Turn right along the gated edge of four fields to a stile. Angle right across the next field, past a low brick structure and down to cross a stile by a tree. Turn left along the hedge, then when it angles left, continue ahead across the large field corner to a waymark post at its wooded

edge. Descend to a footbridge and go up to a stile. Go up the field, over a track and angle right to a hidden stile in the hedge. Turn right round the edge of the next large field to a stile in the top corner. Go slightly left up the field to a stile and across the next two fields to a stile/small gate in the corner.

3 Cross another stile ahead to pass between the tree-covered ramparts of the inturned gateway of Iron Age Caynham Camp into the large grass interior of the fort. Angle right across the fort's interior to a stile and information board. Follow the path down the wooded slope and on to a gate. Go to a wooden gate ahead and down the green track to a stile/gate. In the next field go half-right to a stile, then half-left down the next large field to a metal footbridge alongside water pipes over the river – *the Elan Valley water supply for Birmingham and the West Midlands*. Go slightly right up the field to a stile onto a road. Follow it right with care into The Sheet. Cross to the pavement opposite and continue through the village. Just before the A49 roundabout follow the cycle/walkway to cross the A49 at a

Pelican crossing, then on alongside Sheet Road past Tuffins shop and garage at the outskirts of Ludlow. After the pedestrian crossing turn left on the cycle/walkway signposted to Temeside, soon joining a narrow road which you follow down to a bridge over the railway. At the junction beyond turn right down the road.

At the next junction turn left, soon alongside the tree-lined river Teme. At a T-junction turn left along Temeside. At the next junction turn left near the river. At Ludford Bridge turn right up Lower Broad Street, passing through the old town gate. At the junction at the top turn left along High Street into Market Square.

LUDLOW TO CRAVEN ARMS
10¼ miles

Ludlow is the largest town in South Shropshire. After the Norman Conquest the de Lacy family were given Lordship of an important border manor and chose a good defensive position on prominent high ground near the confluence of the rivers Teme and Corve to build a castle in the late 11thC. It was part of a line of castles built along the Marches to provide a defence against the Welsh. Alongside the castle a town was laid out in a grid network of streets which remain today, and in the 13thC it was enclosed by walls.

From the middle of the 15thC the castle was largely owned by the Crown. In the 1470s it was the childhood home of Edward IV's two sons (of Princes in the tower fame). It then became the administrative headquarters of the powerful Council of the Marches, which governed Wales and the Marches, with features of an Elizabethan mansion. In 1646 it surrendered to Parliamentary forces and by the end of the century it lay abandoned and in decay. In 1811 it was sold to the Earl of Powis and

remains in the family ownership.

Over the centuries the town prospered with weekly markets, becoming a centre for the wool trade and cloth manufacturing, then leather-making. In Georgian times Ludlow became a fashionable social centre.

During much of the 19thC its main industry was glove making, but also textiles, and nail manufacture, then later malting were important. Commerce was boosted by the coming of the railway in 1853 and the town expanded to accommodate a growing population. Fortunately, Ludlow's historic medieval town centre has survived intact. The town's former wealth and prosperity is reflected in its many fine buildings dating from the 16thC. Many visitors are attracted by Ludlow's timeless qualities, its many listed buildings, bustling market, splendid ruined castle, its reputation for good food, and by its horse racing just outside of town, which dates to the early 18thC.

40 Ludlow to Whittytree

6½ miles

After descending from Ludlow castle to cross the river Teme the Shropshire Way begins its journey northwards by field paths and estate road to the attractive hamlet of Bromfield, with the opportunity to visit the nearby Ludlow Food Centre for refreshments. It then continues by field paths and road to the hamlet of Whittytree.

From the Market Square head towards the castle. Just before its entrance turn right and follow the signposted wide stony path round beneath the castle wall, then take a wide surfaced path angling right down through trees to a road. Follow it to a junction then turn right across Dinham Bridge over the impressive wide river – *built in 1823 and offering a good view of the castle.* Continue along the roadside pavement then take the no through road signposted to Priors Halton and The Cliffe Hotel. Shortly, just before the hotel, go through a kissing gate on the right. Go up the field to join the tree boundary, soon

descending to a stile and footbridge over a stream in trees. Cross a nearby stile and turn right up and along the field edge to a stile. Continue along the long field edge beside woodland. Later, as the field narrows, turn left to a stile in the opposite boundary before the field's end. Go down the next field to a stream and a gate beyond. Angle right up the large field to a gate and up the next to a gateway in the corner to reach an estate road beyond. Follow it right down to gates by The Lodge, after which it descends and rises past woodland. The tree-lined road continues to a junction. Keep ahead, shortly descending past a cottage to cross an early 19thC bridge over the River Teme at Bromfield. *The nearby*

former mid 19thC corn mill has been renovated and the weir restored using retrieved masonry from the river, as part of a hydro generation project. The importance of Bromfield's location, lying near the confluence of the Onny and Teme rivers, is evidenced by Bronze Age burial sites and a Roman marching camp. Nearby St Mary the Virgin's church, dating to 1155, was once the chapel of a Benedictine Priory established in 1135 and dissolved in 1540 by Henry VIII. Part of it became

83

a house until it was fully restored in 1658. It contains a splendid painted chancel ceiling dating from 1672. Bromfield is now noted for its Ludlow Food Centre and cafe adjoining the A49 500 metres away.

2 Go through a kissing gate on the left and follow the path near the river to a stile, then along the next field edge, soon bending away from the river. Shortly turn left through a gateway across a stream into the adjoining field. Turn right along its edge. In the corner turn left and follow the field edge to cross a stile by a small lake. Turn left up alongside the hedge, then right along the edge of a long field beside woodland. In the corner turn right and follow the field boundary past Stead Vallets farm to a waymarked gate in it. Turn right along the farm's driveway to the A4113. Cross with care to the opposite side and turn right to a nearby driveway. Follow it to a cottage, then continue to a small gate beyond and along a path to another cottage. Follow its driveway to a road. Follow it right through the small hamlet of Duxmoor, past a side road to Clungunford, to reach a junction at the hamlet of Whittytree.

41 Whittytree to the Discovery Centre, Craven Arms

3¾ miles

This section continues through the edge of parkland and a small picturesque hidden valley to the hamlet of Aldon. It then heads down to Stokesay Castle, a stunning medieval

fortified manor house, well worth a visit, before continuing to nearby Craven Arms.

1 Go ahead past an old telephone box and along a stony track to a gate by an outbuilding. Follow a green track along the part wooded valley past two pools and on to a kissing gate by a third. *These pools formed part of parkland created for nearby Stokesay Court after it was built to replace an existing house in 1889 for John Derby Allcroft, known for his restoration of Stokesay Castle.* Continue along the track through rhododendrons and trees past a fenced game bird area. At the end of the wood go up its left fork, quickly becoming a path, which continues through the edge of woodland to a small gate. Follow the waymarked path through trees to a gateway and on to two finger posts before a small building. Turn right along the bridleway/old green track beneath young trees, shortly bending left into the Aldon Gutter valley. At a track the bridleway continues ahead past an old cottage on the right then a fenced game bird area. At a waymark post by a gate turn right over a stream then left to follow the bridleway up to a gate and a road above. Follow it right past farms in Aldon to a junction. Turn left.

2 Shortly, go along a hedge-lined byway on the right, later descending steadily along the edge of Stoke Wood and on down to cross the railway line. After a farm follow the road past a small lake to the car park for nearby Stokesay Castle and church.

Stokesay Castle is considered to be the best preserved medieval fortified manor house in England. It stands on the site of an earlier house occupied by the de Say family until 1240. The original settlement of Stoke then became known as Stokesay. In 1281 the estate was bought by Lawrence of Ludlow, a rich wool merchant and he built this prestigious country home, with its great hall, surrounded by a moat, now dry. It remained in the Lawrence family for over 300 years. The timber-framed gatehouse was built in 1640-41.

During the Civil War it was garrisoned for the King, but surrendered to Parliamentary troops in 1645. Fortunately only the curtain walls were demolished. For much of the 18thC it was used by tenant farmers, and the buildings fell into disrepair. After decades of neglect it was bought in 1869 by John Derby Allcroft, a wealthy businessman and lovingly restored, then opened to the public in 1908. Since 1992 it has been in the ownership of English Heritage. The nearby St John the Baptist Church, built in 1150, was partly destroyed in the Civil War, and extensively rebuilt in 1654-64. Continue along the road, then just before the A49 turn left along a surfaced path, soon beside the road, then cross to a kissing gate opposite. Follow a path through woodland and on to a finger post, marking the junction of Shropshire Way branches. Follow the path ahead to the Discovery Centre.

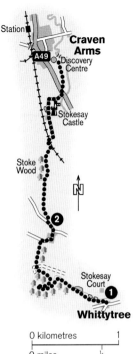

The Shropshire Hills Discovery Centre, open daily, is set in a unique grass roofed building. It is a popular family facility with a gallery, exhibitions, visitor information, organised activities, shop and award winning café.

Craven Arms was originally part of Stokesay township, but developed as a small railway town around a station built on the Shrewsbury–Hereford line in 1852. It took its name from the existing Craven Arms Hotel, lying on the Shrewsbury–Hereford turnpike road. It became an important junction with other new railways to Wellington, Bishop's Castle, and the still existing Heart of Wales line to Swansea, as well as a busy market and livestock auction centre.

85

CRAVEN ARMS TO CHURCH STRETTON VIA WENLOCK EDGE

10 miles

This route uses new sections of the Shropshire Way for a varied walk which takes you to the historic market town of Church Stretton, nestling beneath the Long Mynyd, and from where you can continue to Shrewsbury.

42 The Discovery Centre, Craven Arms to Wolverton Wood

4½ miles

After leaving Craven Arms the route follows field paths up onto a small grass ridge offering extensive views. After a section of quiet road walking via Lower Dinchope, the route follows a delightful bridleway along wooded Wenlock Edge to a junction of Shropshire Way branches at Wolverton Wood.

I Follow a path past the eastern side of the Centre to a finger post, marking the junction of Shropshire Way branches. Bear left along the path signposted to Wilderhope Manor, soon enclosed. Go along a rough lane, then along the narrow road ahead to a footbridge over the river. Go straight across the large field to a stile, then along the edge of the next large field to

a stile onto a road. Cross the stile opposite. Follow the stiled path along a field edge, then ahead up through two fields to the bottom edge of woodland. The waymarked path rises through trees to a stile.

2 Just above turn left along the grassy ridge past a seat, then angle slightly right down the slope, soon joining a narrow faint green track, which descends to a stile/gate. Turn right down the road and continue past side roads. At a junction by Lower Dinchope Farm turn left (Westhope) along the high hedge-lined road, later rising steadily. *Visible on nearby Callow Hill above woodland is Flounders' Folly, a lookout tower*

Wolverton Wood

Strefford Wood

0 kilometres 1

0 miles ½

❶

N

Tower

Lower Dinchope

Craven Arms

Station

B4368

A49

Discovery Centre

❷

built in 1838 by Benjamin Flounders, a prominent Quaker and entrepreneur. After it bends left down to a nearby junction go along the no through road left fork. When it bends right to nearby Moorwood Farm go through a gate ahead and up the hedge-lined waymarked bridleway. Just before a Forestry Commission Strefford Wood board the bridleway bends right and continues along the steep wooded slope of Wenlock Edge. Later, when it splits keep to the left fork. Eventually you reach a finger post at a junction of Shropshire Way sections at Wolverton Wood.

Now follow instructions in **Section 33** from Wolverton Wood to Church Stretton (5½ miles).

CRAVEN ARMS TO CHURCH STRETTON VIA THE LONG MYND

15 miles

This follows the original undulating route, with some minor changes, that features one of the trail's highlights – a great walk along the Long Mynd – combined with a new link via the Carding Mill valley to Church Stretton. The Long Mynd and the Carding Mill valley are probably Shropshire's most popular walking areas.

The Long Mynd is a large expansive upland moorland plateau, about 10 miles long, with steep sided narrow glacial valleys on its east side. It is the most extensive area of open heathland in Shropshire, with its heather and bilberry top a blaze of purple in late summer. Once covered in oak forest, since pre-historic times man has progressively removed trees to create pasture for grazing animals, mainly sheep. Common grazing rights were later established and remain so to this day. It is rich in archaeological remains, including Bronze Age burial sites and Bodbury Ring Iron Age hillfort. It used to be managed as a grouse moor much of it is now owned by the National Trust. Its highest point is Pole Bank (1693 ft/516 metres). It is an important habitat for many bird species, mammals, moths and butterflies.

43 The Discovery Centre, Craven Arms to Hopesay Hill
2½ miles

The Shropshire Way leaves Craven Arms and heads westwards on field paths, later making a long gradual ascent past Sibdon Castle Farm to Hopesay Hill, where the trail splits.

▌At the Discovery Centre entrance turn left to the nearby A49. Go along the footpath opposite (Dodd's Lane) and the road ahead, then an

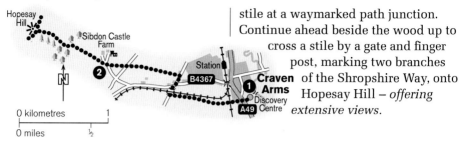

stile at a waymarked path junction. Continue ahead beside the wood up to cross a stile by a gate and finger post, marking two branches of the Shropshire Way, onto Hopesay Hill – *offering extensive views.*

enclosed track under the railway into a field. Continue ahead on the stiled path through two fields, then along the edge of two more by the Heart of Wales railway to a road. Follow it right to a junction. Angle across to nearby bollards, go along a short section of old road, then turn left up another road. Cross a stile on the left by a noticeboard. Follow the path along the edge of three fields, then mid-way in the fourth go through a gate by a stile on the left into the adjoining field. Follow the path up the field edge, then angle left to a stile onto a narrow road. Cross two stiles opposite, then go slightly left up the field past a waymark post by a solitary tree and on up the large field to a kissing gate onto a driveway at the entrance to Sibdon Castle Farm – *an early 17thC fortified manor house.*

2 Go through a kissing gate opposite and over two stiles ahead. Go up the next large field to a stile by a cottage in the top right-hand corner. Continue up through trees, bending left, then go up a field to a stile/gate in its left-hand corner by woodland. Turn left up a faint green track past the wood, then continue up the woodland edge of a large field. In the corner turn left past a small ruined building to a

44 Hopesay Hill to Black Knoll
5 miles

This undulating section now heads northwards, initially rising, then descending in stages, later passing through Plowden Woods, to the Onny valley. Shortly afterwards it begins a long steady climb following a bridleway, an ancient trading route known as The Port Way, up to the top of Black Knoll (1361 ft/415 metres) onto the southern end of the Long Mynd, offering panoramic views.

I Follow the route heading north, signposted Pole Bank/Long Mynd, beside the fence up the hillside, shortly levelling out. In the corner go through the facing of two kissing gates. *Stretching out ahead of you is the Long Mynyd, and to the east the wooded Wenlock edge, with the Clee hills further south.* Follow the green track down to a road. Follow it left down beneath Wart Hill Wood and on past houses and two side roads. The road rises, then descends. Shortly, turn right along a side road to a stile/gate ahead. Go along the field edge and up to a gate at a good viewpoint. Go down the edge of two fields, then descend a steep wooded slope to a gate and on to join a farm track. When it bends left towards a farm go through a waymarked gate on the right and follow the tree-lined path up to an access track to reach a nearby road at Edgton. Go up the narrow road opposite, then through a waymarked gate on the right. Go up a green track along a field edge, then at the entrance to another field go through a small gate on the right. Go up to a stile, then follow the stiled path up the edge of three fields to a small gate into Plowden Woods.

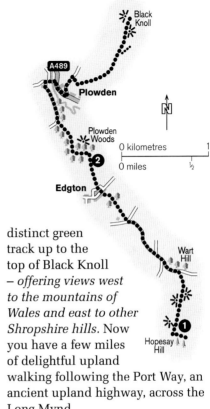

2 Descend to waymark posts and turn left along a wide path on a long steady descent through woodland. On the bend at a junction with a rougher track continue up the main track, past an area of cleared trees – *offering a good view of Black Knoll* – and on to join a stony track to reach a nearby road. Follow it right for nearly ½ mile to a junction. Turn right down the road past a side road and over the river Onny to the A489. Turn right with care along the road, then take a side road on the left signposted to Asterton. After passing through woodland it rises steadily to a cattle grid. Here do a sharp U-turn right onto the signposted Long Mynyd bridleway. After the gate go along the track, soon rising steadily past woodland then another waymarked bridleway into open country to a gate by sheep pens. Continue up the track to another gate. A few yards beyond, the bridleway leaves the stony track and heads up a fainter green track parallel with the fence on your left to go through a gate in it. It then follows a more distinct green track up to the top of Black Knoll – *offering views west to the mountains of Wales and east to other Shropshire hills.* Now you have a few miles of delightful upland walking following the Port Way, an ancient upland highway, across the Long Mynd.

This ancient trackway was probably established during the Bronze Age, over 3,000 years ago as a dry trading route above the then wet and wooded valleys. From the 13thC this section over the Long Mynd was used by drovers taking animals from Bishop's Castle, then later South Wales, to Shrewsbury market. By the 18thC it was a major trading route with considerable movement of livestock and agricultural produce in horse-drawn wagons, which increased further following the opening of the new turnpike road at Church Stretton. With the coming of the railways in the mid 19thC its use rapidly declined.

45 Black Knoll to the top of Mott's Road

5 miles

This section follows the ancient Port Way along the broad Long Mynd ridge, later diverting around the Midlands Gliding Club, one of the oldest in the country with a 334 acre airfield and clubhouse. Gliding began here in 1934 and it is regarded as one of the UK's premier sites. It continues with the Port Way, now a narrow upland road, then heads to Pole Bank (1692 ft/516 metres), the highest point on the Long Mynd, offering breathtaking all-round views. It continues past Shooting Box barrow, a rare Bronze Age burial site named after a grouse-shooting hut that stood on the site, to reach the link to Church Stretton.

1 Follow the green track northwards, shortly rising through heather and bilberry – *with the Stiperstones crags visible to the west* – then continuing through gated National Trust owned Handless beside woodland. Continue along the track. *Don't be alarmed if you suddenly see a glider being launched into the sky, for ahead is the Midlands Gliding Club.* At a finger post marking a crossroad of bridleways go to two finger posts ahead. The Port Way continues ahead, but in order to minimise delays in launching gliders, the Shropshire Way bears left with the signposted permissive Starboard Way. The delightful wide waymarked bridleway curves around the hillside then runs parallel with the nearby Gliding Club's stony track – *allowing you the opportunity to watch gliders taking off and landing on the grass airstrip.* It continues past two small enclosures then the clubhouse.

2 At the fence corner by the windsock the waymarked bridleway continues ahead to the end of the airfield's access road where you rejoin the original Port Way. Continue north along the nearby narrow road, later on a long steady climb. It then passes a small car park before climbing again. Shortly follow a wide bridleway leading left off the road up through heather to a trig point and toposcope on the top of Pole Bank. Continue with the bridleway, over a stony track, and on down to a road by Shooting Box parking area. *Nearby is the ancient disc barrow, the only one in Shropshire.* Follow the wide bridleway ahead through heather, past another bridleway to join a stony track. Follow it to where it splits at a red-topped waymark post. Take the right fork.

Shooting Box

Pole Bank

Gliding Club

2

Long Mynd

0 kilometres   1

0 miles   ½

1

Black Knoll

N

46 Top of Mott's Road to Church Stretton

2½ miles

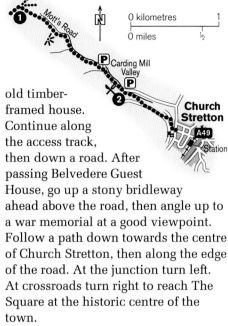

This link section makes a dramatic descent from the Long Mynd down a narrow side valley and through the popular Carding Mill Valley to the historic market town of Church Stretton.

1 After a few yards, when the bridleway splits take the right fork waymarked Pole Bank Walk/ Humphrey Kynaston Way down towards Church Stretton, following a route known as Mott's Road. *This old track is often referred to as Dr Mott's Road, because it was said to be used by doctors from Church Stretton to reach their patients in upland farms.* It then descends more steeply into a narrowing valley. After crossing a side stream continue down the valley to eventually cross a footbridge over the stream by a National Trust car park. *On the nearby hill overlooking the valley is Bodbury Ring Iron Age hillfort.* Follow the road down through Carding Mill valley, shortly using a path to avoid a ford, then rejoining the road. Go past the converted former carding mill factory – *built in the 1820s for cloth manufacturing, then from the 1880s part of it used for ginger beer and soda water manufacture, and a tea-room* – and the current National Trust tea-room.

2 At the coach car park take the waymarked stony bridleway on the right up across the hillside, shortly bending away past The Rowan, an old timber-framed house. Continue along the access track, then down a road. After passing Belvedere Guest House, go up a stony bridleway ahead above the road, then angle up to a war memorial at a good viewpoint. Follow a path down towards the centre of Church Stretton, then along the edge of the road. At the junction turn left. At crossroads turn right to reach The Square at the historic centre of the town.

The area has been occupied by man since the Iron Age, but Church Stretton has its roots in Anglo-Saxon times. It was the largest of three settlements, containing the parish church of St Laurence, that formed the manor of Stretton ('street settlement'), so named because of its location beside the Roman road of Watling Street. It also stood on the Shrewsbury to Bristol road, and an ancient route called The Burway, over the Long Mynd.

After the Norman conquest the manor was held by the Earl of Shrewsbury, then the crown, followed by powerful family dynasties. In 1214 Church Stretton was granted a charter to hold a weekly market and for centuries it has served the mixed farming community, with additional annual fairs for hiring servants, and selling wool, sheep and horses. After

91

a major fire in 1593 much of the town centre was rebuilt. It then became known for its leather trades and domestic weaving of cloth, then larger scale production after the development of the carding mill in the early 19thC until it closed in 1906.
After the coming of the Shrewsbury–Hereford railway in 1852, increasing number of visitors came to the town. They were attracted by its beautiful scenery, which they called 'Little Switzerland', by a climate described as

'invigorating and beneficial to invalids and elderly persons', and by the purity of its natural spring water. By the beginning of the 20thC the town had gained a reputation as a health resort. After the First World War, with the rise in road traffic, the town, Carding Mill Valley and the Long Mynd became increasingly popular with day visitors, as it is today. The Square was created in 1963 on the site of two previous market halls going back to 1617 and still carries on the market tradition.

CRAVEN ARMS TO CLUN
11 miles

An undulating section of the Shropshire Way heading west from the small railway town of Craven Arms to the interesting border town of Clun, the smallest in Shropshire.

47 Discovery Centre, Craven Arms to Lodge Farm
6½ miles

This section first heads westwards, later making a long gradual ascent past Sibdon Castle Farm to Hopesay Hill, where the trail splits. It then follows a new route across Hopesay Hill (931 ft/284 metres), owned by the National Trust and offering great views, down to Hopesay village, with its ancient church and farm tea-room, nestling peacefully in a secluded valley. It then climbs steadily past nearby Burrow Hill Camp, an Iron Age hillfort and descends to Kempton, before crossing

the river Kemp and heading up a side valley to Lodge Farm.
First follow the route instructions in Section 43 from the Discovery Centre to the junction of Shropshire Way branches on Hopesay Hill, then proceed as follows.

I Take the SW route signposted to Hopesay village/Clun, angling left to follow a wide path across the broad top of Hopesay Hill, then descending and passing several wind-battered Scots Pines – *soon with a view of Burrow hillfort and Hopesay village below.* After crossing an old low boundary the wide path descends more steeply to a cross-path at the fence/tree boundary. Turn left to a small waymarked gate, then right to a nearby kissing gate. Follow the path down to a stile and on across the field to a footbridge over a stream. Go along the next field edge to a road. Follow it right into Hopesay to a side road. *A*

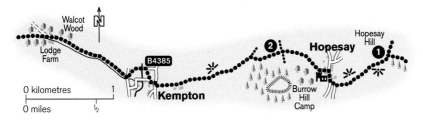

little further along the road is the barn of nearby Hopesay farm, traditionally used by the village as a noticeboard. The village name refers to the valley of Picot de Say, a Norman baron who held the manor. The school, post office and shop have gone, leaving Hopesay as a peaceful backwater. Turn left up the road past the Old Rectory to the late 12thC St Mary's church, where there are information boards about its history. *Sheep are used to graze the churchyard, helping to provide a wildlife habitat. Glebe Farm tea-room is opposite.* Go up the concrete road, then at the top of the churchyard, turn right up a hedged green track to a stile/gate and on to a wood corner. Go up the field edge to a gate in its top right-hand corner. Go up the next large field to a gate and track. *A permissive path leads left to nearby Burrow Hill Camp Iron Age hillfort, one of Shropshire's most impressive.*

2 Go through the gate ahead and follow the gated green track up the edge of two fields, then angle right across the next field corner to a small gate. Turn left along a track (a bridleway) beyond to begin a long steady descent to the B4385 at Kempton. Cross the road and turn right past a lay-by, then sharp left down a narrow road. At a finger post on the

bend by a farm turn right into a short concrete track. Almost immediately go through a waymarked gate and head to a small wooden gate. Go half-left across the large field to a stile onto a driveway. Follow it across the nearby bridge over the river to houses and cross a stile ahead. Angle left to follow a path beside the boundary. In its corner turn right to cross a stile on the left and another ahead. Turn right along a stony track beyond, soon bending past another track and continuing up the valley to Lodge Farm.

48 Lodge Farm to The Square, Clun
4½ miles

The section continues through Walcot Wood, then rises to Bury Ditches (1286 ft/392 metres), an impressive Iron Age hillfort. After descending through the forest it continues to Guilden Down Farm, then heads south to Clun – described by A.E. Houseman in his poem 'A Shropshire Lad' as 'the quietest place under the sun'.

I Soon after gates by an information board on Walcot Wood, angle left off the stony track to follow a green track past the old farmhouse and on through Walcot Wood – *all that remains of*

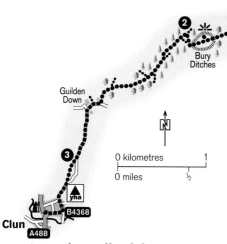

then continue west with the main path through the hillfort, shortly bending through ramparts down to gates. Just beyond turn right along the wide red/blue trail.

2 At a track T-junction turn left. Soon, when the red trail turns left, keep ahead. The track gradually descends through the forest to where it is joined by another track from the left and levels out. Continue with the wide forestry track. At a main track junction keep ahead down the track. After about 40 yards angle left off the track and follow a bridleway down through trees to a gate. It continues along an initially tree-lined track, briefly crosses farmland, then passes through trees past a side track. Shortly the track bends past a house. When it splits follow the one leading left to pass between buildings of Guilden Down. Continue down the minor road southwards towards Clun.

3 After just over ½ mile, at a finger post cross a stile on the right. The stiled path angles left across and down two fields, then round to the entrance of Mill Barn. Go down its access track, then continue up the road past the youth hostel – *a former mill, once powered by water from a lake.* Soon the road bends left past the Memorial Hall car park in Clun. At the next junction follow the road ahead (Hospital Lane) past Trinity Gardens and chapel – *worth a visit to see the 1614 almshouses and sculptures of almsmen* – to the High Street. Turn right past side roads

ancient oak woodland that was once a large Elizabethan deer park. When it does a sharp U-turn right follow a waymarked path ahead up through trees to join a green track above. Follow it left to a gate by another information board then up above the stream past woodland. When it bends left go through a small gate ahead to a house. Go up its access track, then turn right up a road and into the entrance of Bury Ditches car park. Take a path on the right past a Welcome board and up to a path junction. Go up the blue/red trail path ahead to a small gate into the hillfort. *The full scale and detail of the fort were only revealed in 1976 after trees were blown down by storms and subsequent clearance work by the Forestry Commission. The Iron Age hillfort, with its classic inturned entrance, was defended by substantial ramparts and ditches.* Follow the path up through the ramparts to a path junction at a board depicting how the hillfort might have looked. First divert right up to a toposcope at the northern ramparts to enjoy extensive views,

View from Hopesay Hill

to a junction. Keep ahead along the A488 to The Square, once the bustling centre of this small former market town. Nearby is the very interesting Clun Museum, which opened in 1932 in the former town hall built in 1780 and later used as a courthouse and a gaol, then market hall. It contains the original curator's amazing collection of pre-historic tools and flints. (It is open Easter – 31st October, Tuesdays, Saturdays and Bank Holiday Mondays.)

Clun has its roots in an ancient Saxon settlement clustered around a 7thC church near the river of the same name, but it is essentially a planned Norman town. After the Norman Conquest, Clun became the centre of a large Marcher lordship with a castle and a growing town, whose grid pattern layout of streets remains today. It was granted its town charter in the 14thC.

It was on an ancient drovers' route along which cattle were taken from Wales to the Midlands and London, and for centuries was a thriving market town, serving a large area. During the 19thC it was known for its shoemaking, with many craftsmen engaged in this trade. It was the only town in Shropshire not connected to a railway and subsequently its prosperity declined. The oldest part of the town is around St George's Church, built by the Normans on the site of the Saxon church. Now it is a quiet charming rural community, which comes alive each May during the Green Man Spring Festival celebrations.

The original motte and bailey castle was built by Robert de Say and strengthened during the 12thC as a defence against the unruly Welsh. It was then largely owned by the powerful Fitzalan family, who used it as their main residence until they acquired the wealthier Arundel Castle in Sussex. It was in action during Owain Glyndŵr's early 15thC rebellion against English rule but by the mid 17thC it had been abandoned. The castle is said to be the scene of Sir Walter Scott's novel 'The Betrothed'.

95

CLUN TO BISHOP'S CASTLE
11¼ miles

49 The Square, Clun to above Churchtown
5½ miles

After visiting Clun castle the trail heads north west across country, then makes a steady climb along the Cefns, a delightful ridge, offering great views, reaching a height of 1213ft/370 metres. It descends to Three Gates Farm, crosses the shoulder of Hergan hill at 1279 ft/390 metres then follows an undulating section of Offa's Dyke Path north to just above the hamlet of Churchtown.

I From The Square follow the road as it bends north. Soon turn left along a track signposted to the Castle. After visiting the ruins return to the access gates and cross a nearby stile. Go along the path to a house, then an access track past others. Continue along a hedge-lined path, then beside the stream to a footbridge over it and a stile into a field. Go along its tree-lined edge to a footbridge and stile, and on to cross a stile in the boundary by the stream. The path follows the boundary to a nearby stile, then moves away from the stream between hedge and tree boundaries and continues by the hedge to stiles. Follow the delightful tree-lined path to a road.

2 Cross the stile almost opposite and go up the field edge, then where the ground levels out the waymarked path angles right across the field to a stile/gate. Go along the next field edge to a stile/gate, then at a nearby gate to the left in trees turn right up a stiled tree-lined path. Now follow a stiled path along and up the edge of five fields on the Cefns – *meaning ridge in Welsh and said to be an old drovers' road* – then along the next at the highest point of the broad ridge to a stile/gate. Angle left down the field to a stile, then go ahead along the next field

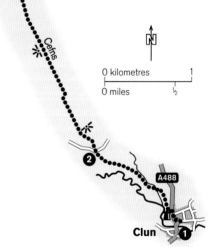

edge to a small gate. Go through the gate ahead and follow the enclosed green track down to a road. Follow it past Three Gates Farm, then at crossroads go up the road ahead.

3 Take the signposted path on the right opposite farm buildings to a stile/gate by the house. Go up the tree-lined path to a stile and on up to a gate..Go up the edge of two fields onto Hergan, then half-left across the next large field to join a green track near a gate in the far boundary. Follow it westwards down to a kissing gate/gate. *Prominent in the valley below is the unmistakable line of Offa's Dyke.* Continue along the track to a finger post, where you join the Offa's Dyke Path. Do a sharp U-turn right, signposted to Churchtown, down a green track to pass through a gap in the dyke. Turn left down beside it to a stile. Continue briefly beneath the dyke, then cross a stile on its top. Follow the stiled field path beside the western side of the dyke, shortly descending to a footbridge over a stream, then rising to a small gate. Go along the field edge past a barn to another small gate. Cross the nearby house's driveway and follow the Offa's Dyke Path down to the dyke/boundary below. The path descends between the two, crosses a stream and rises beside the initially Scots pines covered dyke to a lane. Go through the kissing gate opposite. Follow the dyke down to another kissing gate, then more steeply down through mixed woodland to a finger post just above a small gate, where the Offa's Dyke Path continues down to nearby Churchtown – *a small hamlet in a secluded valley containing St John the Baptist church, built in 1887 on the site of an earlier church.*

50 Above Churchtown to the Town Hall, Bishop's Castle
5¾ miles

The trail now heads eastwards into the Unk valley, then climbs again before descending to Middle Woodbatch Farm and continuing to the historic market town of Bishop's Castle.

1 The signposted Shropshire Way now turns right up through trees and continues along the bottom edge of conifers then across the deciduous tree-covered slope to a narrow road. Follow it down to a junction in the valley by houses. Turn right past Cow Pasture Gate, then just beyond, cross a stile on the right. Turn left, moving away from the boundary, to follow a path through the middle of the large field to a stile into mixed woodland. The path rises through trees, then follows a level wider path through the wood. At a waymarked path junction go down the left fork to a road by the River Unk. Follow it left to a junction. Go through the kissing gate opposite and up the enclosed sunken bridleway to gates. Turn briefly up a stony track to a finger post. Now follow the bridleway up the old sunken green track. Just before a gate in the boundary ahead, turn right along the top field edge up to gates. Now follow the gated tree-lined bridleway on a long steady climb across the hillside, then continue along a house's access track to a road. Turn left.

2 After a few yards turn right through a gate into a field. Follow the farm track past a barn, then along the edge of the large field, soon bending right with a view down to Bishop's Castle. Before reaching the

Bishop's Castle

Middle Woodbatch Farm

A488

Churchtown

1

2

N

3

0 kilometres   1

0 miles   ½

field corner turn left down to a nearby stile/gate. Go down the field then turn right alongside the fence, soon angling left with it down a tree-lined bridleway to a gate. The bridleway continues down the edge of a wood to a stony track. Follow it right down through Middle Woodbatch Farm then continue down its access track, shortly levelling out and becoming a road. Later it bends left down to cross a stream. Just beyond cross a stile on the right. The stiled path follows the stream through five fields to the waymarked corner of sheep pens near a stile and gate at the stream.

3 Here turn left up the field slope passing to the right of a small quarry to a fence corner and a stile in the corner beyond. Go along the edge of the next two fields, then follow a green track along another field. Continue along a narrow hedge/tree-lined path, then across an open aspect. Go past houses, then follow the access track to a road in Bishop's Castle. Follow it left past the fire station and nearby St John the Baptist Church, with its original Norman tower, to a junction. Turn right and at the next junction left towards the town centre.

At crossroads keep ahead up Church Street, then High Street to the Town Hall, with its prominent clocktower – *the focal point of the town's political, economic and social life since the mid 18thC.*

Bishop's Castle was originally an Anglo-Saxon settlement but after the Norman Conquest the Bishops of Hereford were appointed Marcher Lords responsible for the defence of the border with Wales here. They built a motte and bailey castle between 1085-1100 at the top of the hill, below which, by the mid 12thC, a small town had been laid out leading to the church – hence its name. In 1167 a stone castle replaced the original and was strengthened in 1281. The town received a Royal Charter in 1249 to hold a weekly market, which is still held every Friday, and trade flourished. The town lay at the eastern end of an ancient upland trading and droving route from Wales, known as the Kerry Ridgeway, along which livestock were brought to market. In 1573, the town became free of the control of the Bishops, under a new Royal Charter from Elizabeth I which allowed self government by a Borough Council. By the mid 17thC the castle was a ruin and now Castle Hotel occupies the site. The town, along with others, became notorious for its bribery in the election of its two MPs, which it lost under the Reform Act of 1832.

In 1865 it was connected by a railway to Craven Arms and used to transport cattle, goods and passengers. The company quickly ran out of money, were unable to extend to Montgomery, and for most of its existence, until it closed in 1935, the line operated under an Official Receiver.

BISHOP'S CASTLE TO BRIDGES
12 miles

51 Town Hall, Bishop's Castle to Linley Hill
4¾ miles

The trail heads across farmland to Lydham then passes ancient castle earthworks near More, a hamlet with an unusual 13thC church, well worth a short detour. After passing through Linley, with its nearby 18thC hall, the route rises steadily up a splendid beech-lined green track onto Linley Hill (1296 ft/395 metres).

From the Town Hall continue up the High Street. When the road bends right into Salop Street keep ahead up Bull Lane. Near the top the signposted Shropshire Way turns left up a path between houses, then a track to the Bowling Club – *said to have existed since the 17thC.* Continue along the narrow path ahead between houses. At the road turn right to a nearby junction. Go along the left-hand pavement, then turn left along a track between houses to a small gate ahead by a garage. On a rise just beyond, at a path junction, turn right along a tree-lined path to a kissing gate. The path continues across

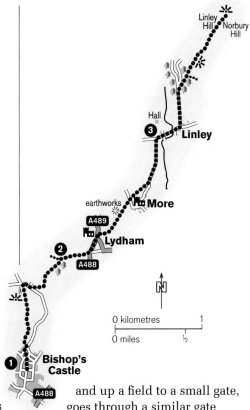

and up a field to a small gate, goes through a similar gate in the next field corner, passes a Buddha sculpture and seat, then continues up by the hedge. Soon turn left through a gateway just before a

99

The Shropshire Way

house, then right along the field edge
down to a stile. Follow the path down
the large field to a road junction. Turn
right, then from the entrance to Upper
Heblands Farm follow the signposted
trail across the field to its far left-
hand corner and through trees into
the next field. Turn left past a finger
post and follow the bridleway along
the large field edge, soon bending
right and descending. Midway at a
post the bridleway leaves the field
and continues between a hedge and
a fence. It then briefly passes through
mixed woodland before angling left to
a small gate. Go down the field/wood
edge to gates.

2 Follow the hedge-lined track
ahead to the A488. Turn left along
the grass verge, then pavement to the
A488/A489 junction in Lydham by
nearby 13thC Holy Trinity church.
Just beyond the junction cross the
road and go along the left-hand side of
the Village Hall car park to a kissing
gate. Head up the field, past a double
telegraph pole, to a kissing gate in
the corner into a large field. Pass just
to the left of a large tree ahead and
follow the path to a footbridge in the
boundary. Go along the next field edge
past earthworks of a motte and bailey
castle. *Little is known about its history,
but it is believed to be early 12thC.*
Soon angle away from the fence and
continue to the right of telegraph poles
through more earthworks to a gate onto
a road. *Nearby is More, an attractive
historic late 11thC village of timber-
framed houses and 13thC St Peter's
church, with its double pyramidal
17th C roof and floor tiles by the font*

100

*from a Roman villa found near Linley
Hall.* Go through the gate opposite and
follow a stiled path across three fields
to another road. Follow it left.

3 At the junction – *with 18thC Linley
Hall ahead* – turn right along the
road past Oak Avenue, the 17thC
driveway to Linley Hall, over the river,
then in the hamlet of Linley, turn left
up a road signposted to Cold Hill/The
Bog. When it splits at woodland go
up a track on the right along the wood
edge. When it bends right to a gate
continue up a green track to a stile/gate
at the wood corner. Go up the majestic
mature beech – lined green track –
possibly planted in the early 18thC
– later gradually fading and levelling
out at a second gate. Continue ahead
between the last line of trees. Ignore a
path angling right but go across upland
pasture to a stile/gate ahead. The path
now continues up between the top of
Linley Hill and Norbury Hill to a gate
at its highest point – *offering a great
view of the Stiperstones.*

52 Linley Hill to Bridges link, Stiperstones
4½ miles

After descending into a side valley, the
trail rises again to continue through
two distinctly different parts of the
Stiperstones, a stunning heathland
ridge, offering great views. Its southern
section, Nipstone Nature Reserve, has
been cleared of conifers to provide a
better habitat for wildlife. The northern
section is internationally famous for its
quartzite outcrops rising to 1759 ft/536
metres, the second highest point in

Shropshire. It is now a National Nature Reserve providing a varied heathland habitat for various endangered species including red grouse, snipe, raven, common lizard and emperor moth. It is undoubtedly one of Shropshire's wildest places and the route across it, known as the Stiperstones Stomp, is spectacular. However care is needed crossing its boulder covered terrain, especially in poor visibility. Land below the western side of the Stiperstones was once extensively mined for lead, dating to Roman times. To learn more about its history and enjoy great home-made cakes, it is recommended that you make a short diversion down to the Visitor Centre in the former school of The Bog lead mining village demolished in 1972.

1 Continue along the broad ridge, soon descending to a stile/gate. Keep ahead along the wide path near the fence, soon bending down to a stile/gate. The trail now heads west by the fence past a conifer plantation to a stile/gate. Angle slightly right down the hillside (not down into the side valley) then follow the boundary on the right down to a gate onto a road..Follow it right past the nearby farm. Just after it bends right cross a stile on the left. Follow the path down the increasingly tree-covered slope to stiles and a footbridge, then up the large field to a stile by houses

onto their access road. Turn right then after a few yards left up a track through woodland. Soon take the waymarked path angling left up through an area of young trees to gates at a great viewpoint looking south. The wide path continues up through an area of cleared forest to pass through a gap in the ridge beneath 'The Rocks' – *the rocky end of Nipstone Nature Reserve.*

2 At the top, with new views west, turn right, soon taking the stonier right fork through heather. When it splits follow the waymarked left fork to a stile/gate on the wide heather ridge. Continue with the path, shortly passing Nipstone Rock at the northern end of the ridge to a stile/gate. Go across a track to a kissing gate at the corner of the pine wood ahead by an information board. Follow the stiled path through the wood edge, then go across the large field past a line of trees to a finger post. (For the Bog Visitor Centre turn left to a kissing gate and follow the path down the field to another. Continue down a narrow path to a small pool and site of the mid 19thC lead mine, which closed in 1922. Descend to the car park below, then go down the road to the Visitor Centre. Retrace your steps.)

3 Continue to the nearby road. Go through the kissing gate opposite and another ahead to enter Stiperstones National Nature Reserve.

Manstone Rock, Stiperstones

Follow the path to a waymarked path/ bridleway junction. Keep with the path up through heather past the first group of rock outcrops, then head up to its highest known as Cranberry Rock. From its northern end a stony path continues along the broad heather ridge. At a stone cairn it is joined by a bridleway coming in from the right and the wide stony path continues northwards past other rock outcrops to the highest on Stiperstones, trig point topped Manstone Rock. Follow the wide stony path to the last razor like outcrop called the Devils's Chair – *which is the subject of local folklore and has featured in several literary works.* It now begins a long gentle descent north east through heather to a stone enclosed waymark post at a cross track/path intersection, with scattered stone outcrops ahead.

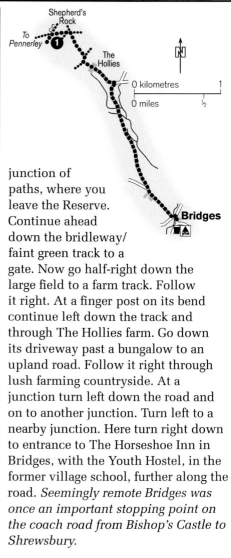

53 Stiperstones To Bridges
2¾ miles

The section now leaves Stiperstones Nature Reserve and heads south east down to the hamlet of Bridges, nestling in the East Onny valley between Stiperstones and the Long Mynd.

▌ Turn right and follow the narrow track down to a stile/gate at a

junction of paths, where you leave the Reserve. Continue ahead down the bridleway/ faint green track to a gate. Now go half-right down the large field to a farm track. Follow it right. At a finger post on its bend continue left down the track and through The Hollies farm. Go down its driveway past a bungalow to an upland road. Follow it right through lush farming countryside. At a junction turn left down the road and on to another junction. Turn left to a nearby junction. Here turn right down to entrance to The Horseshoe Inn in Bridges, with the Youth Hostel, in the former village school, further along the road. *Seemingly remote Bridges was once an important stopping point on the coach road from Bishop's Castle to Shrewsbury.*

BRIDGES TO SHREWSBURY

16 ¾ or 15 miles

OR CHURCH STRETTON

7 miles

From Bridges the Shropshire Way heads north east to the Port Way, an ancient upland route, then offers a choice. The main original route continues north to Shrewsbury, while a new branch heads east to Church Stretton.

54 Bridges to the Port Way

2½ miles

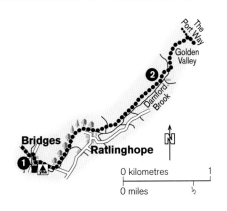

The trail continues up a valley between Ratlinghope Hill and the Long Mynd, passing the ancient hamlet of Ratlinghope, then rises to meet the Port Way (see page 89 for information) and splits.

1 From the Horseshoe Inn go along the road past the youth hostel. Just before the river cross a stile on the left. Follow a green track through. woodland near the river. At a small bridge over it cross a stile up on the left. The stiled path follows the river along the valley beneath conifers, then deciduous woodland to a footbridge and ford opposite a large house in the hamlet of Ratlinghope – *originally a Saxon settlement and the site of a small early 13thC Augustian priory and St Mary's church. Its churchyard contains the 1906 grave of a local farmer said to be England's last sin-*

eater – an ancient custom involving someone paid to eat bread and drink ale over the body of a person who had died suddenly to take away their sins. On Ratlinghope Hill are the remains of two earlier Iron Age settlements, the most notable – Castle Ring. The trail now follows a narrow green track then path for almost a mile along the more open Darnford Brook valley to a stile/gate opposite Lower Darnford Farm.

2 At a fingerpost beyond turn left up a track to a nearby gate. Follow the level green track to a stile/gate by a finger post. Go past the tree ahead to cross a stream. At a waymark post beyond turn left up the path to a stile. The path continues across upland pasture known as 'Golden Valley' then rises steadily to a kissing gate onto the Port Way.

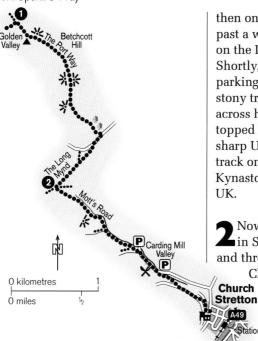

then on to join a more substantial track past a wood to reach an upland road on the Long Mynyd. Follow it right. Shortly, turn left across a small rough parking area and go along a straight stony track, soon joined by another, across heather moorland. At a red-topped bridleway waymark post do a sharp U-turn left along another stony track on the waymarked Humphrey Kynaston Way/Pole Bank Walk/Ride UK.

2 Now follow the route instructions in Section 46 down Mott's Road and through Carding Mill Valley into Church Stretton.

55 The Port Way to Church Stretton
4½ miles

This new link follows the Port Way across Betchcott Hill, offering extensive views, to a road on the Long Mynd, then descends Mott's Road into Carding Mill Valley to reach Church Stretton.

Turn right through a nearby gate and follow the enclosed track up to a gate by a small building. Follow the fence past a trig point and along the large field across Betchcott Hill. In the corner go along a short fenced green track to a gate. Follow the gated green track by the fence up the edge of two fields, along the next to pass small plantations and a small pool,

56 The Port Way to Exford's Green
6½ miles

This section begins the trail's journey northwards to Shrewsbury. It first follows an upland road, then crosses Wilderley Hill, offering panoramic views, before making a long gradual descent in stages across attractive countryside to Wilderley Hall Farm. It continues across farmland to the hamlet of Exford's Green, where it is joined by the new Shropshire Way branch from Stiperstones.

Go up the stony track, signposted to Shrewsbury, then continue along the road. At a junction go through a kissing gate ahead. Go across the field to a small inscribed stone, then half-right to two small gates in the boundary. Angle left across the upland pasture of Wilderley Hill past a small fenced enclosure to a great viewpoint. Go down a green track past a conifer wood, then follow its perimeter fence down to gates at the bottom. Follow a path down the edge of the large rough field, at a cross-path bending left and continuing near the tree boundary to a kissing gate into another field. Follow the old tree boundary up to a good viewpoint and on to a small kink in it. Here turn sharp right across the field to the hedge opposite, then follow it left to a bridle gate onto a nearby farm's access track. Go through a bridle gate ahead and down the edge of the long field. Go past a gate just before the corner and keep ahead down narrow tree-lined rough ground to a gate. Go along the short enclosed bridleway, then a farm track to a road by Wilderley Hall Farm – *all that remains of the medieval hamlet of Wilderley, once overlooked by a Norman motte and bailey castle – whose remains are nearby.* Turn right along the road, then take the left fork (Stapleton) past houses and Lane Farm. Later the road bends northwards.

Map labels:
Exfords Green
Lower Common
The Vinnals
Cottage Farm
Wilderley Hall Farm
N
0 kilometres 1
0 miles ½
Wilderley Hill
Golden Valley

2 Soon after passing Keeper's Cottage and just before outbuildings of Cottage Farm turn left through a kissing gate and cross the field to a footbridge into another field. Join the tree boundary ahead and follow it round to a footbridge, then go along the next field edge to a road. Turn right, then left through a nearby kissing gate. Go along the edge of two fields to a road, then follow the path opposite past a wood, and up the field to the right-hand corner onto an access track. Go along the tree/hedged-lined bridleway ahead, then a track to The Vinnals farm. Follow its access track/road to a junction. Turn right to a kissing gate at the end of bungalows. Go along the narrow enclosed path to another kissing gate. Turn right along the edge of a long field to a kissing gate by a former 19thC chapel at the small community of Exfords Green. Follow. the enclosed path to join Hurst Bank's access track by a track junction.

57 Exford's Green to Rea Brook, Shrewsbury
4¼ miles

This section takes you across Lyth Hill, famous for its ropemaking in the 18th and 19th centuries, and now a Country Park. Despite only 534 feet/163 metres high it offers panoramic views. The route later passes through Bayston Hill to reach Rea Brook at the outskirts of Shrewsbury.

1 Go down the straight tree/hedge-lined stony track to a road. Turn left, then soon right on the signposted bridleway along a stony track past two houses, shortly bending right below a large house. When it bends left follow the gated bridleway ahead up past a seat, then up a field edge. It passes between Coppice Gate Cottages and continues up the stony access track past other houses, including Windmill Cottage – *with the 1830s windmill behind it.* Take its right fork to Lyth Hill Heritage Site car park. Go along a track, soon joining a stony one, which continues past access points onto the adjoining open hillside (an alternative route) to another car park. *This track was used to stretch and braid rope made here, and is still called the Rope Walk.*

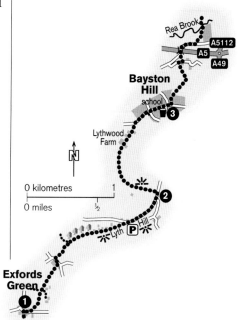

2 Turn left along the road, then take a narrow path on the left past a fenced covered reservoir, then go slightly left across the large field to a kissing gate/gate – *enjoying a first view of Shrewsbury.* Follow a track between fields and through Lythwood Farm. Continue along its access road past two houses. At a house on the right turn left through a gap in holly then follow an enclosed path past allotments. Go through a car park, then follow a road to a junction. Turn right through an estate at the outskirts of Bayston Hill. At crossroads continue along the road ahead to the Beeches pub. *This part of Bayston Hill dates from the 1960s but its origins are ancient. The older village lies just to the east of the A49 around The Common and near the remains of an Iron Age hillfort and a Roman settlement.*

3 Cross to Oakmeadow School entrance opposite and continue along the pavement past Landsdowne Road (shops). Turn left along the next road (Castle Lane), then follow an enclosed path past The Castle. Follow a path ahead through the field then left along the edge of the next field round to a stile. Go along the next field edge to a road. Follow it right to a kissing gate on the bend. Turn left along the field edge to another road. Follow it over the A5 then shortly turn left on the signposted SW to a kissing gate. Go along the field edge, then just before the corner turn right along a narrow enclosed path, past a side path, then down to cross a large footbridge over Rea Brook at the outskirts of Shrewsbury. Soon, at a waymark post, you have a choice of routes into the centre of Shrewsbury.

58 Rea Brook to The Square Shrewsbury

Route A 3½ miles

A new waymarked meandering route passing through sections of Shrewsbury Town Council's Rea Brook Valley Local Nature Reserve, now a haven for wildlife and flowers, but with a long tradition of corn milling. This attractive hidden green corridor follows Rea Brook right into the heart of the town to emerge by the Cathedral.

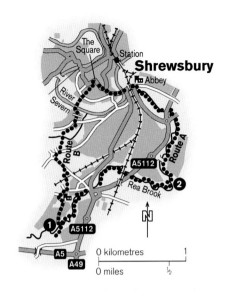

1 At the waymark post turn right and follow the path through woodland near Rea Brook, go up steps then turn right along a fenced path to cross a large footbridge over the river. Turn left behind bungalows and continue near the river through woodland, across a footbridge over a stream and on to a kissing gate. At a nearby road leading to a large roundabout, turn left along a cycle/walkway, passing under bridges over the river then rising to the roundabout. Go through a kissing gate on the left and along a path, then briefly the edge of a golf course, before descending a path through trees. Cross a golf link then bend right along the riverside edge of the golf course. After passing through trees go across a golf link to a waymark post. Follow the path near the river, passing under the railway bridge, then the A5112 road bridge. Soon turn left along the narrow stony waymarked path through trees, over a footbridge and on back to rejoin the river. After crossing a footbridge over it take the railed path down to a picnic table by the river. Continue with the waymarked route through Rea Brook Reserve, later passing a children's play area, then crossing a footbridge.

2 At a crossroad of paths turn right to cross a large iron footbridge over the river. Descends steps and continue on the right bank of the river. After passing under an old railway bridge follow the path's left fork by the river, on past houses, and through a field. Continue through trees along the riverside edge of another field. *Ahead is Lord Hill's column built in 1814-16 to honour Shropshire's most distinguished soldier. He was the Duke of Wellington's most trusted and respected general in the Peninsula War and at Waterloo, known as 'Daddy Hill' by his troops. It is the tallest Greek Doric column in England.* The path passes under a road bridge, continues by the river, then angles away from it through a field and passes under another road bridge. It then bends left up through trees and continues along

The Square, Shrewsbury

a section of a former railway line. Just before a car park turn right to a kissing gate and follow the stony path through a field to another. Continue along the surfaced path past Asda and a car park to a road and cross to Shrewsbury Cathedral opposite. Turn left along the pavement, under the railway bridge, and on across the English Bridge over the river Severn. Go along the road, bending up Wyle Cop past Dogpole street then along High Street to The Square.

Route B 1¾ miles

This follows the original, but more urban, direct route to the centre of Shrewsbury. It has been retained as Route A is susceptible to flooding after heavy rain.

1 From the waymark post follow the path ahead, over a bridge and up to a Church Road. Go up the road, later bending left past the church and a recreational area. At the junction go ahead along Vicarage Road, then turn

left along Meole Walk. Very soon turn right along an enclosed path between houses, then cross the railway line with care. Turn right and follow the edge of a large sports field round to take a waymarked path up to Roman Road. Continue along the cycle/walkway up to a roundabout. Turn right across Roman Road then continue along the nearby side road (Longden Road).

2 At the entrance to the cemetery cross to a short narrow hedged path opposite. Continue down the path through trees, across a bridge over a stream, and up to a path junction. Turn right along the wide path behind houses, then along a stony track (Beehive Lane). At the junction go along the road opposite, under a bridge, and on to cross Kingsland Toll Bridge over the river Severn. At crossroads continue ahead along Swan Hill, past the Coach and Horses and the Admiral Benbow pubs, descending to a junction by Loch Fyne seafood restaurant. Turn right then left to the Old Market Hall in The Square.

STIPERSTONES TO SHREWSBURY
18 or 16¼ miles

59 Bridges link, Stiperstones to Pontesford Hill

6½ miles

This section gradually descends the northern end of the Stiperstones ridge, then passes through woodland above Snailbeach, containing preserved relics of the area's important lead-mining past. After passing through Maddox Coppice and Poles Coppice Nature Reserve, it heads eastwards to follow a bridleway around the lower wooded slopes of Earl's Hill Nature Reserve, then Pontesford Hill.

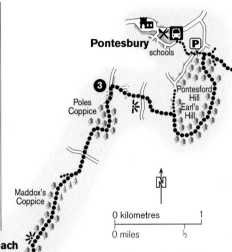

I Follow the stony bridleway ahead to another small cairn at a waymarked crossroad of bridleways and path, near Shepherd's Rock. (The green bridleway leading left descends into a side valley to Stiperstones village.) Continue ahead with the wide bridleway – *as it begins to descend enjoying a good view into an impressive side valley and ahead to distant Earl's Hill.* Shortly after being joined by a track from the left by a fence/tree boundary, and before the bridleway bends left, at a post, angle left down a path. Soon it passes below a fence and above a steep wooded side valley. After a small gate the path

continues down the field edge, then bends left past another side valley and down past a large barn to a kissing gate, now briefly leaving Stiperstones Reserve. Go half-left across upland pasture and down to a kissing gate. Follow the path down through woodland past an information board by a path to nearby Resting Hill chimney – *which connected with a long underground flue from a lead smelter at Snailbeach Mine in the second half of the 19thC –* then the remains of an impressive Victorian Cornish Engine House to a road. *The area has been mined for lead since Roman times and it became one of the country's most productive, with underground mining ceasing in 1955.* Turn right up the road.

109

2 On the bend follow the signposted SW left up through the wood, along the edge of a large field, then another wood edge. The path shortly descends, becoming a narrow stony track, then continues down through Maddox's Coppice, passing mountain bike trails. At a track T-junction turn right, then soon left on a path up through trees. Follow the tree-lined path to a road. Continue along a tree-lined track opposite, then across a field to the corner into Poles Coppice Nature Reserve – *an ancient oak woodland containing disused 18thC stone quarries.* Turn right and follow a waymarked path down the wood edge, then northwards through the Reserve, soon joined by a bridleway, to emerge from the trees by a small car park. Follow the road ahead, soon descending.

3 At the bottom turn right on the signposted bridleway along a stony track. Just before Nills Farm it angles to a small gate and passes the house, then through trees. It continues down between houses and along an access track to a road – *with a good view ahead of Earl's Hill, of volcanic origins, on top of which is a small Iron Age hillfort.* Follow a green track opposite, then in the field corner turn right along its edge to a stile. Go along the edge of two fields up to a hedge-lined track at the wooded corner of Earl's Hill Nature Reserve – *Shropshire Wildlife Trust's first in 1964.* Turn right on the bridleway along the wood edge. At a gate, where it splits, the Shropshire Way turns left up through the wood, levels out and continues along the wood edge to a bridle gate. After passing another

waymarked bridleway it reach another bridle gate and information board. The gated bridleway now descends an open area, then continues along the bottom wooded edge of Pontesford Hill, shortly descending.

60 Pontesford Hill to Exford's Green

3¾ miles

This section goes across attractive part wooded countryside containing several small pools, to the old village of Longden, before continuing across farmland to the hamlet of Exford's Green, where it joins the main branch of the Shropshire Way heading to Shrewsbury.

I When the bridleway bends left to a car park go down the path ahead to a small gate. Go across the field to another small gate, then turn right up the stony track. At the entrance to The Fishpools turn left through a kissing gate. Follow the path to another kissing gate and across the next field to a small gate in the corner. Go along the next field edge to a small gate and another beyond. Angle left past a waymarked fence corner to a stile. Go across the field to a kissing gate and follow the gated path down through a wood to cross a footbridge over the river. Soon turn left along a waymarked bridleway up the wood edge, then right up a stony access track to a road. Follow it left past two cottages then by the third turn right up steps to a small gate. Go along the field edge, through the wood past Lincroft Pool, then along the bottom field edge by trees. With another pool ahead turn right up a narrow rough track. Go along the left-hand field edge then just before a sleeper bridge/stile at a wood perimeter, turn left beside the fence, soon bending left to a kissing gate/

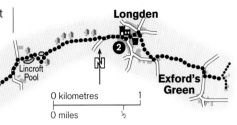

gate. Continue along a faint track above a stream, then turn right across a sleeper bridge over it. Turn left along the wood/field edge to a gate. Go along the edge of two fields, then a green track to a road. Follow it left into Longden.

2 At the junction turn left past 16thC St Ruthen's church, then the Tankerville Arms and a post office/shop. At crossroads turn right along School Lane, then immediately right along the signposted path past tennis courts and a children's play area to a stile. Go down the field edge to a stile/footbridge/stile. Enter a field ahead then go slightly right up to the waymarked tree boundary corner Turn left to a stile and left along the enclosed farm track

to cross a stile just before a road, and another nearby. Go along the field edge past an old corrugated barn, then a gate in the hedge. At a waymark post angle right across the field past a boundary corner and on beside the hedge to a stile. Go up the left-hand edge of the large field to a road. Turn right then cross a stile on the left. Follow the fence up the field to cross a stile in the adjoining tree boundary. Angle left across the field corner to a kissing gate and go across the next field to a stile in the left-hand corner and a kissing gate onto Hurst Bank's access track at Exford's Green. Turn left to the adjoining track junction.

Now follow instructions in **sections 57** and **58** to the centre of Shrewsbury.

CHURCH STRETTON TO SHREWSBURY

18¾ or 17 miles

61 The Square, Church Stretton to link to Bridges

4½ miles

This section follows a new branch of the Shropshire Way from Church Stretton through Carding Mill Valley, then up to an upland road on the

expansive heather covered Long Mynd at 1574 ft/480 metres. It then follows the Port Way, an ancient upland trading route (see page 89 for information) across and down enclosed upland pasture, then Betchcott Hill to a junction of Shropshire Way routes. Please refer to the map on page 104. For information on Church Stretton see pages 91-92.

Mott's Road

From the Square continue along High Street to crossroads by HSBC bank. Turn left up Burway Road then at crossroads turn right up the left-side grass edge of Longhills Road. Soon follow a path up to a memorial cross and a seat, then down to follow a stony bridleway through trees, and continue up the road. After a cattle-grid take the stony access track angling right to The Rowans, then follow a bridleway into impressive Carding Mill Valley down to a road. Follow it up the valley past the National Trust tea-room, then converted factory – *built in the 1820s for cloth manufacturing, then from the 1880s part of it used for ginger beer and soda water manufacture, and a tea-room.* Use the footpath to avoid the ford and continue up the road. At the car park entrance turn left across a footbridge over a stream. Follow the wide stony path above the stream on a long steady climb up the valley to cross a side stream. Continue up the stony bridleway ahead, signposted 'Shooting Box', climbing more steeply up the more enclosed valley. *You are following an ancient route known as (Dr)*

Mott's Road, said to have been used by doctors from Church Stretton to reach their patients in upland farms. Later, continue up a narrow stony track onto the Long Mynyd. Eventually it levels out at another track/bridleway coming in from the right. Bend left to a nearby wide stony cross-track at a waymarked bridleway junction. Turn right.

2 Follow the wide stony track north eastwards through heather. When it splits, keep ahead to a road. Follow it right. Just before a cattle-grid turn sharp left along a stony track to a gate and on past woodland. Continue ahead along a gated green track near the fence, past small plantations and a pool, then shortly descending two fields. The track continues between fences then along a large field edge across Betchcott Hill past an aerial and trig point to a small building. Go down the part stony enclosed track to a gate and the signposted link route to Bridges beyond.

Now follow sections **56 – 58** of the Shropshire Way to Shrewsbury.

Multi-day long distance walks

The Shropshire Way, with its numerous linked sections, offers great potential for long distance walks of varying length to suit individual needs, including fitness and time available.

All Shropshire trail (200¾ miles)

This is the longest continuous multi-day Shropshire Way route around the county. It links Shrewsbury, Llanymynech, Chirk Bank, Ellesmere, Whitchurch, Wem, Wellington, Ironbridge, Much Wenlock, Widerhope Manor, the Clee Hills, Ludlow, Craven Arms, Clun, Bishop's Castle, Stiperstones, Bridges and Exford's Green (sections 1-4, 7-13,15-17, 21-23, 26-30, 34-37, 39-41, 47-54, 56-58). There are various permutations for a shorter circuit – eg. taking the Montgomery Canal route direct to Lower Frankton, missing out Whitchurch or the Clee Hills etc.

North Shropshire

There are several variations on a circular route around North Shropshire, starting and finishing at Shrewsbury. Routes A and B use an additional section of the Llangollen Canal, not designated as part of the Shropshire Way network, to enable the inclusion in the circuit of the historic market town of Whitchurch and the attractive links to it.

Route A *(98½ miles)*

This route links Shrewsbury, Llanymynech, Chirk Bank, Ellesmere, Whitchurch, Wem and Haughmond Abbey (sections 1-4, 7-13, 15-20).

Route B *(84¾ miles)*

This route follows Route A to Llanymynech, then the alternative scenic Montgomery Canal link to rejoin Route A at Lower Frankton (sections 1-6,11-13, 15-20).

Route C *(85¾ miles)*

This route follows Route A to Whixall Marl Allotment then misses out Whitchurch and heads direct to Welsh End Junction, where it rejoins Walk A (sections 1-4, 7-14,17-20).

Route D *(70¾ miles)*

This route follows Route B to Whixall Marl Allotment, then misses out

Whitchurch, and heads direct to Welsh End Junction, before continuing via Wem to Shrewsbury (sections 1-6, 11-14, 17-20).

The trail can be undertaken as two shorter separate walks linked to rail or bus services – e.g. Shrewsbury to Whitchurch and Whitchurch to Shrewsbury. Another delightful varied circular walk is to follow the route from Llanymynech to Chirk and along the Llangollen Canal to Lower Frankton, returning along the Montgomery Canal.

The route south east from Wem to Isombridge Farm then west to Shrewsbury is too long for a day's walking. However, an alternative from Wem is to follow new links to Wellington (sections 21-23 & 26) and either take a train/bus back to Shrewsbury or join the Shropshire Way (South) circuit.

South Shropshire

There are also several variations on a circular walk around South Shropshire, starting and finishing at Shrewsbury.

Route A *(119¼ miles)*

This route links Shrewsbury, Wellington, Ironbridge, Much Wenlock, Wilderhope Manor, the Clee Hills, Ludlow, Craven Arms, Clun, Bishop's Castle, Stiperstones, Bridges and Exford's Green (sections 24-30, 34-37, 39-41, 47-54, 56-58).

Route B *(118 miles)*

This route links Shrewsbury, Wellington, Ironbridge, Much Wenlock, Wilderhope Manor, the Clee Hills, Ludlow, Craven Arms, Clun, Bishop's Castle, Stiperstones, Pontesford Hill, and Exford's Green (sections 24-30, 34-37, 39-41, 47-52, 59-60, 57-58 in order of travel). Note this will be dependent on staying 1 mile off the route at Stiperstones Inn, reached by a bridleway from near Shepherd's Rock, mentioned in paragraph 1 of section 59, or Bridges and rejoining it the next day.

Route C *(102 miles)*

This route links Shrewsbury, Wellington, Ironbridge, Much Wenlock, Wilderhope Manor, the Clee Hills, Ludlow, Craven Arms, Hopesay Hill, Long Mynd, Church Stretton, and Exford's Green (sections 24-30, 34-37, 39-41, 43-46, 61, 56-58).

Route D *(97 miles)*

This route links Shrewsbury, Wellington, Ironbridge, Much Wenlock, Wilderhope Manor, the Clee Hills, Ludlow, Craven Arms, Church Stretton and Exford's Green (sections 24-30, 34-37, 39-41, 42, 33, 61, 56-58).

All these routes can be shortened using the new links from Wilderhope Manor on Wenlock Edge to Craven Arms or Church Stretton, which omit the loop via the Clee Hills and Ludlow to Craven Arms.

Imaginative use of route sections can be used to create various other short multi-day walks linked to rail or bus services – eg. Shrewsbury to Ironbridge; Ironbridge to Ludlow; Ludlow to Church Stretton via Craven Arms, Clun, Bishop's Castle and Bridges. A Craven Arms-Church Stretton circular walk is another suggestion for a long weekend break. Perhaps better to stay in Church Stretton, take the train or bus to Craven Arms, then return separate days by the Long Mynd and by Wenlock Edge carrying only a day bag.

Linear day walks

Most of the Shropshire Way can be undertaken as linear day walks of varying length, linked to public transport. This enables people to enjoy the new walking opportunities offered by the extended Shropshire Way at convenience and over time. The only part of the route where the lack of public transport makes this not possible is that from Much Wenlock via Wilderhope Manor and the Brown Clee Hills to Coldgreen (sections 30, 34-35). However this can be undertaken using two cars, or as a two day walk.

As a general rule when using a car and public transport for a linear walk, especially if it is a long one, it is better to leave your car at the finish of the walk, then take a bus or train to the start point. In that way you can enjoy the walk at your own pace without the pressure of having finish by a specific time for a bus or train. However routes linked to trains, which tend to run later than buses, offer more flexibility, and some walks comfortably use public transport in both directions.

Bus services in particular can change at any time, so please check current available services and timetables before planning any walk. Visit the website www.travelshropshire.co.uk which has a link to www.travelinemidlands. co.uk for transport information, inc. timetables, location of bus stops etc.

I have identified 33 main walks following the Shropshire Way around the county, a few with additional shorter route options. Use the buses or trains indicated then follow the appropriate sections of the Shropshire Way.

1 Shrewsbury to Montford Bridge (7½ miles)

Park in Montford Bridge (large lay-by at northern end of village). Take ½ hourly no. 70 bus to Shrewsbury bus station. From The Square follow section 1 back to Montford Bridge.

2 Montford Bridge to Pines car park, Nesscliffe Countryside Heritage Site (8 miles)

At the Three Pigeons in Nesscliffe on the A5 take the road opposite up past St.Andrew's School then Oakes car park to a junction. Turn right up the road, then left along a track to Pines car park. Return to the A5 to catch ½ hourly no.70 bus to Montford Bridge. Follow section 2 back to Nesscliffe, then paragraph 1 of section 3.

3 Nesscliffe to Llanymynech (14 miles)

From the car park in Llanymynech, behind the Dolphin Inn return to the A483 and turn right to a bus stop opposite The Bradford Arms Hotel. Take no. 71/X71 bus to Oswestry bus station, then the no. 70 bus to The Three Pigeons in Nesscliffe. Continue along the road, then follow section 3 to Llanymynech.

4 Llanymynech to Queens Head, on the A5 (6¾ miles) or the Narrowboat Inn on the A495 near Welsh Frankton (12 miles) or Ellesmere (14 miles)

From Oswestry bus station take the no. 71/X71 or 72 bus to Llanymynech. Walk section 5 to Queens Head and catch the no. 70 bus to Oswestry. Option 2 continue with section 6 along the Montgomery canal to Lower Frankton, then follow the Llangollen canal to the Narrowboat Inn. Catch the 449 bus to Oswestry. Option 3 continue with section 11 to Ellesmere and catch the 53/449 bus to Oswestry. Another option is a walk from Queens Head to Ellesmere (7 ¼ miles), using the 70 bus from Oswestry and the 53/449 from Ellesmere for the return.

5 Llanymynech to Oswestry (10 miles)

From Oswestry bus station take bus no. 71/X71 or 72 to Llanymynech. Follow section 7 to Candy Woods, then the described link to Oswestry.

6 Oswestry to Chirk (14 miles)

Use the large car park behind The Hand Hotel, Chirk. From St.Mary's church bus stop in the main street catch the 2/2A bus to Oswestry bus station, then follow this described link to Candy Woods to join the Shropshire Way.

Go past Aldi, then turn left along the road, past Morrisons garage and on along the no through road ahead past shops, soon bending left. At crossroads turn right along Cross Street, then go along Church Street to St Oswalds' church. From its main door take the pathway to the 1631 lychgate by the Visitor and Exhibition Centre. Follow a walled path to the road. Follow it right over Welsh Walls, then turn right along Oswald Place. It soon becomes Oswalds Well Lane and passes Brynhafod Playing field. Continue up Maserfield past the site of Oswalds Well through the estate. At its end turn left along a lane to a road. Turn right up it, then cross a stile at the end of Rose Cottage. Go along the large field edge and past the boundary corner to a small tree ahead. Just beyond bear right along a faint green track to a road. Follow a track opposite through a large field, later bending right up its end to a large tree. Go to a stile/gate ahead into woodland. Follow the path to a path junction. Turn left, soon through trees, to a stile/gate. Nearby is a large old walled garden. Go across the field and through a gate. Keep ahead to follow a faint green track across estate land to a kissing-gate to pass behind a house. Continue along its stony access track. Just after a building it descends. As it begins to bend left follow a waymarked path straight ahead along the bottom edge of woodland/rhododendron, passing above a house, then bending right to a signposted crossroad of paths, where you join the ODP/SW. Now follow sections 8 and 9 to Chirk Bank, then the link to Chirk.

7 Chirk Bank to Ellesmere (9¾ miles)

From Ellesmere take the 53 bus to Oswestry bus station, then the 2/2A to Chirk Bank. Follow sections 10 & 11 to Ellesmere.

8 Ellesmere to Whitchurch (14½ miles)

From Shrewsbury take the Bryn Melyn bus 501 to Ellesmere. Follow sections 12,13 & 15 to Whitchurch. Take a train to Shrewsbury.

9 Ellesmere to Wem (14 ¾ miles)

From Shrewsbury take the Bryn Melyn bus 501 to Ellesmere, then follow sections 12-14, 17 to Wem. Take a train to Shrewsbury.

10 Grindley Brook to Whitchurch (2¼ miles)

From Whitchurch bus station take the 41 bus to a stop adjacent the Horse & Jockey on the A41 at Grindley Brook. From the car park entrance cross the road to the garage entrance opposite and follow a signposted bridleway along a stony lane to bridge 28 over the Llangollen Canal. Follow the canal south via the staircase locks to the junction with the Whitchurch branch, then paragraph 2, section 15 into Whitchurch.

11 Whitchurch to Wem (13½ miles)

From Wem take the 511 bus from the church to the bus terminus in Whitchurch by Tesco's. Turn left past cash machines, then follow a pedestrianised street ahead to a road. Follow it left to the town clock. Alternatively, from Wem railway station take a train to Whitchurch. Turn right up Station Road. At crossroads go down Green End opposite to reach the town clock. From the town clock follow sections 16 & 17 back to Wem.

12 Wem to Shrewsbury (16½ miles)

From Shrewsbury take the 511 bus trom Shrewsbury bus station to the town church in Wem. Alternatively take a train to Wem. Go through the car park on its western side and head into the town centre to the Castle Hotel. Follow sections 18-20. This route can be undertaken as 2 shorter walks: Wem-Hadnall (7 miles) and Hadnall-Shrewsbury (9½ miles) using the 511 bus. Other walks include from the Dog in the Lane pub, Upper Astley – Shrewsbury (7 ½ miles), using bus 64 and Haughmond Abbey-Shrewsbury (4½ miles), using bus 519, and Wem - Grinshill - Clive (5½ miles) using bus 511.

13 Wem to High Ercall (13¼ miles)

From High Ercall take the 519 bus to Shrewsbury, then bus 511 or train to Wem. Follow sections 21, 22 and paragraph 1 of section 23.

14 High Ercall to Wellington (7 miles)

From Wellington take a train or bus 81 to Shrewsbury, then bus 519 to High Ercall. Follow paragraph 2 in section 23 to Isombridge Farm, then section 26 to Bowring Park, Wellington. For the town centre continue along the road.

15 Wem to Wellington (20 miles)

From Wellington take a train or bus 81 to Shrewsbury, then a train or bus 511 to Wem. Follow sections 21-23 & 26.

16 Shrewsbury to Wellington (14¼ miles)

From Wellington take bus 81 or a train to Shrewsbury. Walk to The Square, then follow sections 24-26 to Bowring Park, Wellington. For the town centre continue along the road.

17 Wellington to Ironbridge (11 miles)

From Ironbridge take bus 96 to Shrewsbury, then a train or bus 81 to Wellington. From the railway station head along the road signposted to the town centre. At the junction turn left, then bend right along the left-hand side of Market Street. At traffic lights cross Bridge Road to the pavement opposite and turn left. Soon turn right along Haygate Road. Cross to the opposite side to just before the entrance to Bowring Park. Follow sections 27 & 28 to Ironbridge.

18 Ironbridge to Much Wenlock (4½ miles)

From Much Wenlock take bus 18 to The Square, Ironbridge, then follow section 29. This can also be done from Shrewsbury, taking bus 96 to Ironbridge and returning on bus 436.

19 Coldgreen to Angel Bank (6 miles)

From Ludlow take early morning 141 school bus to Coldgreen, opposite Three Horseshoes Inn on B4364. Return ½ mile along the road with care, then follow sections 36 & 37 to the A4117 at Angel Bank. Turn right along the pavement down past Angel House. Cross to the junction/turning for Knowbury, from where you catch the 2L bus to Ludlow.

20 Clee Hill via Titterstone Hill to Cleobury Mortimer (9 miles)

From the High Street, Cleobury Mortimer take the 2L bus to Clee Hill Stores in Clee Hill village. Go briefly back up the road and along The Crescent opposite. At the T-junction turn right up the road, then left along a former railway line, then descend between houses to a road at Dhutstone. Turn right up it. Shortly, take a signposted bridleway along a track on the left and down to Nine Springs Farm/Cottage. Go to a stile/gate below the house, where you join the SW. Follow the waymarked bridleway down the field edge ahead to a small gate, down to a footbridge over a stream, over a nearby access track and on across open ground to an underpass bridge. Climb up its left-hand side then turn right on a long steady climb up the former quarry incline.

At the top follow the waymarked SW path angling right across a large level old quarry area, past a large concrete structure, then left up a narrow stony track and through a stone-clad gap in a bank ahead. Just beyond angle left up to a road, with Titterstone Hill quarry car park nearby. Go to the twin waymarked SW post opposite and over the road above. Follow the waymarked SW up a narrow stony track, then along the rim of the extensive quarry up to the trig point on Titterstone Clee. Return to the twin waymarked SW and follow section 38 to Cleobury Mortimer.

21 Angelbank to Ludlow (5½ miles)

From Ludlow take the 2L bus to Angel Bank, alighting opposite the road to Knowbury. Follow the pavement up past Angel House to a side road on the left, then follow section 39. A slightly shorter alternative is to follow the Knowbury road through Fardon, then after the driveway to New House Farm, join the signposted SW on the left at paragraph 2.

22 Ludlow to Craven Arms (11 miles)

From Craven Arms take bus 435 or train to Ludlow, then follow sections 40 & 41. The route can be undertaken as two shorter walks, to and from Bromfield, using the 435 bus and/or Castle Connect shuttle.

23 Craven Arms via Wenlock Edge to Church Stretton (9 miles)

From Church Stretton take bus 435 to alight just before the Discovery Centre, Craven Arms or a train (free car park at station) to Craven Arms. From the railway station turn right along a surfaced path parallel with the railway, then turn left across a car park and past a garage to the main road. Follow it to a roundabout by the Craven Arms Hotel and continue ahead along the A49 to the Discovery Centre. Follow sections 42 & 43.

24 Craven Arms via Long Mynd to Church Stretton (15 miles)

Instructions as Walk 23 to the Discovery Centre, then follow sections 43-46.

25 Craven Arms to Clun (11 miles)

From Clun catch the first Castle Connect Shuttle bus 783 to Ludlow. Take bus 435 or a train to Craven Arms. From the Discovery Centre follow sections 47 & 48 to Clun.

26 Clun to Bishop's Castle *(11¼ miles)*

From Bishop's Castle catch the Castle Connect Shuttle bus 783 to Clun. Follow sections 49 & 50. Alternatively take the twice monthly Tuesday bus 860 (call 01588 640273 M&J Travel for details).

26 Bishop's Castle to Pontesbury *(16½ miles)*

In Pontesbury turn off the A488 along Chapel Street signposted to Habberley.. Turn left along the next road signposted to the library to find roadside parking by the cemetery. Return to the A488 and turn right past Connections café and Pontesbury Public Hall to a bus stop. Take the first bus 553 to Bishop's Castle, then follow sections 51, 52 & 59. Follow the bridleway bending left to Earls Hill nature reserve car park. Turn left along the road, then take the second signposted path on the right below a cottage down to a building, over an access track, across a field, then turn right along a driveway to a road. Follow it left past Mary Webb School & College, the Primary School and Library to the cemetery.

27 Stiperstones village to Pontesbury *(11 miles)*

Park in Pontesbury as in Walk 26 and take bus 552 to the school (last stop) in Stiperstones village, then follow the road to the Bog Visitor Centre. Go up the road to a car park at the old lead-mining site, then either continue up the road or follow a waymarked link path up to join the SW. Follow paragraph 3 of section 52, then section 59 across Stiperstones ridge. Follow the described link route in 26 to Pontesbury.

28 Stiperstones to Pontesbury *(8¾ miles)*

From Carding Mill Valley or Beaumont Road, Church Stretton take the shuttle bus 780 to Stiperstones car park. Walk further along the road to join the SW at the entrance to Stiperstones Nature Reserve, just beyond the road junction. Now follow paragraph 3 of section 52, and section 59 across Stiperstones ridge and on to Pontsford Hill. Follow the described link route in 26 to Pontesbury, to catch the shuttle bus back to Church Stretton.

29 Stiperstones to Snailbach *(4 miles)* or **Habberley** *(5¾ miles)*

Follow the first two sentences in Walk 28, then paragraph 3 of section 52, and paragraph 1 of section 59. Follow the road down to Snailbeach and its fascinating old lead-mine to catch the 780 shuttle bus back to Church Stretton. For the longer walk continue with paragraph 2 of section 59, passing through Maddox's Coppice to a road. Follow it right to The Mytton Arms in Habberley, to catch the shuttle bus back to Church Stretton.

30 Pontesbury to Shrewsbury *(12¾ miles)*

From Shrewsbury bus station take bus 552/553 to alight on the A488 opposite The Nag's Head pub, on the eastern outskirts of Pontesbury. Walk back along the pavement and turn right along the road signposted to Pontesford Hill/Earl's Hill nature reserve to enter the small reserve car park. Follow a bridleway east, then when it bends right turn left down a path to a small gate. Follow sections 60, 57 & 58 to Shrewsbury.

31 Bayston Hill to Shrewsbury *(4¾ miles)*

From Shrewsbury bus station take frequent 27 bus to alight near the Beeches pub in Bayston Hill. Follow paragraph 3, section 57, then Route A in section 58.

32 Bridges to Church Stretton *(7 miles)*

From Carding Mill Valley or Beaumont Road, Church Stretton take the shuttle bus 780 to Bridges, then follow sections 54-55 back.

33 Church Stretton to Shrewsbury *(19 or 17¼ miles)*

From Shrewsbury take a train to Church Stretton, cross the footbridge and follow the station road to the main road (Sandford Avenue). Follow it past shops to crossroads by HSBC bank, then follow sections 61, 56-58 back to Shrewsbury.

Guidance Notes and Useful Information

General advice

In this book I have divided the Shropshire Way into 61 short sections. These cover all current 27 linked routes of the official trail, with the exception of the link from Cleobury Mortimer to the Severn Way, and include my own new link along the Llangollen Canal to Whitchurch. I have put them in a more logical numerical sequence reflecting clockwise circuits around both north and south Shropshire. Each section contains detailed route descriptions, accompanying maps and notes on local history and places of interest. This will help you to choose or link sections to meet your own personal requirements for day or multi-day walks.

For those wishing to undertake the trail as a continuous multi-day walk, the daily stages will be determined as much by available accommodation on or near the trail as by level of fitness. It may be that you end a stage where you can catch a bus or train to available accommodation and return the following day to continue the trail. It is recommended though that accommodation, especially where limited or in high summer, is booked in advance.

Given the good public transport system that supports much of the Shropshire Way, it is possible to undertake a multi-day trip without carrying a full pack. From one or two accommodation bases, especially Shrewsbury, and using a combination of car, bus and train you can complete sections carrying only a day bag. I would particularly recommend this approach to those people wishing to camp – a method I have used successfully to complete several long distance walks. The section detailing linear day walks linked to local buses and trains will help in your planning.

Undertaking sections of the trail as day walks can be done throughout the year, with daylight hours of winter dictating shorter distances. For those planning continuous multi-day walks, the best time is between Spring and late Autumn. Each season offers its own appeal. In Spring the trees and hedgerows are returning to life, the woods are full of bluebells and wild garlic, and birdlife is particularly active. Summer with its long hours of daylight and sunshine allows more time to enjoy the scenery. The changing colours of Autumn are delightful, especially along Wenlock Edge.

Whenever you choose to walk the trail please remember to build sufficient time into your itinerary to visit and enjoy the many places of interest along the route. Good walking boots are required along with appropriate warm and waterproof clothing to protect against the elements. The hills are magical on a sunny day, but more challenging when rain and mist quickly descend. Be prepared for any weather, which can vary from Spring snow on the hills to hot Summer sunshine, when you will need suntan cream. Remember that all day walking in the sun unprotected can cause discomfort and be harmful. Carry plenty of drink and food, especially on those sections where facilities are limited or non-existent, as well as emergency equipment, including compass, whistle and small torch, plus OS map. Please note that mobile phone signals can be unreliable, especially in upland areas. For many sections of the Shropshire Way you may walk all day without seeing many people, especially other walkers.

The Shropshire Way uses the county's extensive Rights of Way network of paths, bridleways, and byways, as well as quiet country roads, permissive paths, canal towpaths, recreational trails, and Open Access land. Please remember that changes in details on the ground - i.e. new kissing gates, field boundaries, path diversions etc can occur at any time. Also be aware that the condition of paths can vary according to season and weather. In high summer crops will be at their highest, and stiles can sometimes be hidden by overgrowth. Generally I found that farmers had left clear paths through crop fields. However be prepared for occasions when you have to walk around the field edge or use roads to bypass a path blocked by crops. Modern farming methods have resulted in some very large fields, so carefully follow my instructions to navigate the correct route.

If you encounter any problems on rights of way or with other aspects of the trail please report these to Shropshire Council's Outdoor Recreation Team. Visit www.shropshire.gov.uk/outdoorrecreation or ring 0345 678 9000.

Shropshire Walking website

This website www.shropshirewalking.co.uk is a good source of information, with links to other key websites, and provides news and updates. It contains a specific section devoted to the Shropshire Way, which provides details of route sections, including downloadable maps and town street plans. It is where you should check for any route changes or the current status of sections awaiting upgrading and waymarking. I reported a few minor inaccuracies between the highlighted route on its maps and the waymarked route on the ground, so read my instructions in conjunction with any signage/waymarking.

The current 27 route sections on the website correlate to the following sections in this guidebook: *Route 1* (51-53); *Route 2* (49-50); *Route 3* (47-48); *Route 4* (40-41); *Route 5* (36, 37, 39); *Route 6* (34-35); *Route 7* (31, 33); *Route 8* (54-55); *Route 9* (44-45); *Route 10* (31-32); *Route 11* (38); *Route 12* (30); *Route 13* (29); *Route 14* (59-60); *Route 15* (56-58); *Route 16* (26-28); *Route 17* (24-25); *Route 18* (21-23); *Route 19* (1-2); *Route 20* (3-4); *Route 21* (18-19); *Route 22* (16-17); *Route 23* (12-14); *Routes 24 & 25* (7-9); *Route 26* (10-11); *Route 27* (5-6).

Maps

The route is covered by the following Ordnance Survey maps:

1:50000 Landranger: 117, 126, 127, 137, 138.

1: 25000 Explorer: 201, 203 , 216 , 217 , 240, 241, 242, 257.

Note that OS maps may not yet have been updated to reflect changes to the original Shropshire Way route or to show new route sections.

Waymarking

The new Shropshire Way still carries the original buzzard logo. The new attractive waymarks are a directional arrow (path/bridleway/byway) with the logo in the centre. Where the original waymarks remain the head of the buzzard indicates the direction to follow.

Whilst the Shropshire Way is a long distance walking trail promoted by Shropshire Council, reflecting years of planning and execution, its development has been phased, dependent upon accessing funding – more difficult during years of austerity. Most of the South Shropshire route has been upgraded and newly waymarked, with sections 24-25 awaiting completion. More work remains to be done in North Shropshire. There is currently no SW waymarking on sections 1-4 and it is limited or intermittent on sections 17-19, and 21-25, although new kissing gates have been installed in places. These sections pass through farming country so it is important to follow the detailed route instructions in conjunction with maps.

Facilities

The Shropshire Way passes through market towns and villages that offer a variety of facilities. For the long distance walker the main considerations are overnight accommodation, evening meal options and refreshment stops/shops on or near the route. The internet is a good source of information for planning your walk. For general information, including details of all Visitor Information Centres and accommodation visit www.shropshiretourism.co.uk.

Shropshire has a high number of towns with accredited 'Walkers are Welcome' status. These currently include Church Stretton, Clun, Bishop's Castle, Ludlow, Cleobury Mortimer, Much Wenlock, Wellington, Ironbridge, Oswestry and Whitchurch.

The following information is a guide, but inevitably details will change. More information on specific named places (B&Bs, pubs, cafes etc) can be found online. If planning to call at a pub on route I advise you contact it in advance to check its opening times and whether it serves food.

Shrewsbury to Llanymynech

Shrewsbury offers a full range of facilities. Montford Bridge has the Wingfield Arms pub and recommended Severn House camp site. Nesscliffe has the Three Pigeons pub and a chinese restaurant. The nearest B&B off the route is Hollies Farm, Little Ness. Later on the route is the Royal Hill pub and campsite, Edgerley. Big Bear Lodge offering B&B and camping lies just off the route south of Melverley Green. There is a campsite by Melverley Church. Llanymynech has B&Bs, eating options, and a shop.

Llanymynech to Chirk Bank or Lower Frankton

Trefonwen has the Barley Mow pub and nearby Lynstead Lodge B&B. Glan-yr-Afon, Candy on the route offers B&B, evening meals, and camping with breakfast. Oswestry offers full facilities. Chirk Bank has the Poacher's pub just south of canal bridge 19W. Chirk has B&Bs, eating options and shops. The Montgomery canal section has a tea-shop at Canal Central, the Navigation Inn at Maesbury Marsh and the Queens Head pub by the A5.

Chirk Bank to Ellesmere

The route passes the Jack Mytton Inn at Hidford and The Narrowboat pub at the A495. Ellesmere has B&Bs, eating options and shops, with a campsite at nearby Newnes.

Ellesmere to Whitchurch

There are no facilities until Whitchurch, which offers various including camping by the canal (www.hadleycrosscountry.com) and at the Marina.

Whitchurch to Wem

On the route at Prees Heath is the Raven Hotel, offering B&B and food, cafes, fish & chips, convenience stores. There is camping at Abbey Green farm, Whixall. Wem has eating options, shops, limited B&Bs & Lower Lacon camp site outside the town.

Wem to Shrewsbury

Tilley has the Tilley Raven pub and Grinshill, has The Inn at Grinshill offering B&B. Hadnall has The New Inn, Saracens restaurant and B&B, and a convenience store. Upper Astley has The Dog in the Lane pub. There is a campsite at Ebury Hill. Hot & cold drinks are available from Haughmond Abbey reception. There is the Corbert Arms in Uffington.

Wem to Wellington

There is the Stanton Arms pub in Stanton upon Hine Heath and the Cleveland Arms and a shop in High Ercall..The route passes Allscott Mill B&B, the Plough Inn at Cross Green and Church Farm B&B, Wrockwardine. Wellington offers B&Bs, eating options and shops.

Shrewsbury to Wellington

Haughmond Abbey offers hot & cold drinks. There is a café (open daily) at Haughmond Hill site and the Bull's Head pub in Roddington.

Wellington to Ironbridge

Wrekin Cottage on the climb up The Wrekin offers drinks & snacks. In Little Wenlock, The Huntsman pub offers food and B&B. Ironbridge has B&Bs, youth hostel, eating options, and small store.

Ironbridge to Wilderhope Manor

Much Wenlock has B&Bs, eating options and shops. There are no facilities along Wenlock Edge, except camping at Lower Hill Farm below it. Wilderhope Manor is a youth hostel, providing meals.

Wilderhope Manor to Ludlow or Cleobury Mortimer

Holy Trinity Church in Holdgate offers walkers a coffee-making facility. Between the Brown Clee and Titterstone Clee hills the route passes Upper Bromdon B&B. There is Angel House B&B at Angel Bank, with camping at New House Farm, Fardon, and a store and fish & chips at Clee Hill village. On section 38, there is The Crown pub at Hopton, then B&Bs, eating options, and shops at Cleobury Mortimer. There is nothing on section 39 until you reach Ludlow, which offers many facilities.

Ludlow to Craven Arms

There is a tea-room inside Stokesay Castle at weekends when open and a café at the Shropshire Hills Discovery Centre, Craven Arms (open daily).
There are B&Bs, eating options and shops at Craven Arms.

Craven Arms to Church Stretton

On the eastern route there is B&B at Acton Scott Heritage farm. On the western route along the Long Mynd, there is Glebe Farm run tea-room in Hopesay village and a National Trust tea-room in Carding Mill valley. Church Stretton has B&Bs, camping, eating options and shops.

Craven Arms to Clun

The Hopesay Glebe Farm tea-room is the only facility until Clun, which has B&Bs, a youth hostel with camping, eating options and shops.

Clun to Bishops Castle

Apart from Middle Woodbatch Farm on the route, which offers B&B and camping there are no facilities until Bishop's Castle, which has B&Bs, camping, eating options and shops.

Bishops Castle to Bridges

Just off the route is a recommended café at the Bog Visitor Centre. Bridges has a youth hostel with camping, and The Horseshoe Inn (better known as 'The Bridges') offering B&B & food.

Bridges to Shrewsbury

This section has Lane Farm B&B, Wilderley and Lyth Hill House B&B, then at Bayston Hill, the Beeches pub and shops.

Stiperstones to Exford's Green

Stiperstones village off the route has the Stiperstones Inn, offering B&B, food and a shop. In Longdon there is The Tankerville Arms and a shop. Pontesbury has pubs, café & a shop.

Transport

Shropshire has a good public transport infrastructure of buses and regular main line rail services. Shrewsbury is its main hub and easily accessible via the National Rail network from any part of the UK including a direct service from London. Various railway lines connect Shrewsbury with the county towns of Wem, Whitchurch, Wellington, Church Stretton, Craven Arms and Ludlow.

Key bus services currently supporting the Shropshire Way are:

70 Shrewsbury–Oswestry, calling at Montford Bridge, Nesscliffe and Queens Head.

2/2A Wrexham–Oswestry, calling at Chirk and Chirk Bank.

71/X71 Welshpool–Oswestry (Tanat Valley Coaches), calling at Llanymynech and Llynclys.

72 Llanfyllin–Oswestry (Tanat Valley Coaches), calling at Llannymynech.

53 Ellesmere–Oswestry

449 Welshampton–Oswestry, calling at Ellesmere and Welsh Frankton.

501 Shrewsbury–Ellesmere (Bryn Melyn).

511 Shrewsbury–Whitchurch, calling at Hadnall, Clive (opp post office) and Wem.

519 Shrewsbury–Newport, calling Uffington adj. Haughmond Abbey and High Ercall.

64 Shrewsbury–Market Drayton, calling at Astley (Dog in the Lane).

81 Shrewsbury–Telford, calling at Wellington.

96 Shrewsbury–Ironbridge (Bryn Melyn).

18 Telford–Much Wenlock, calling at Ironbridge.

436 Shrewsbury–Bridgnorth (GHA Coaches), calling at Much Wenlock.

141 Ludlow–Bridgnorth (R&B Travel school bus), calling at Horseshoes Inn, Coldgreen on B4364

2L Kidderminster–Ludlow (Diamond Bus), calling at Cleobury Mortimer, Clee Hill and Angel Bank.

435 Shrewsbury–Ludlow (Minsterley Motors), calling at Church Stretton, Craven Arms and Bromfield.

553 Shrewsbury–Bishop's Castle (Minsterley Motors), calling at Pontesbury.

552 Shrewsbury–Stiperstones (Minsterley Motors), calling at Pontesbury and Snailbeach.

(Bus services are operated by Arriva Midlands unless where stated.)

Shropshire Hills Shuttle bus services

There are two shuttle bus services serving the western Shropshire Hills operating *every weekend and Bank Holiday Mondays from the beginning of May until the end of September.*
Visit www.shropshirewalking.co.uk for more information, including timetables.

The Castle Connect Shuttle (service **783**) connects Ludlow, Bromfield, Knighton, Clun & Bishop's Castle.
The Long Mynd & Stiperstones Shuttle (service **780**) links Church Stretton, Bridges, Stiperstones, Snailbeach, Pontesbury and other places. It offers great walking opportunities for walkers.

Visit www.travelshropshire.co.uk or www.travelinemidlands.co.uk or www.nationalrail.co.uk for public transport enquiries.

Please remember that bus services *are limited on Sundays.* They are all subject to timetable or operator changes, especially with local authority budget cuts, so always check in advance.

The Countryside Code

Be safe – plan ahead and follow any signs

Leave gates and property as you find them

Protect plants and animals, and take your litter home

Keep dogs under close control

Consider other people

In addition respect any ancient site visited.

Other Kittiwake Guides by David Berry

Available at local bookshops and Tourist Information Centres,
or online at: www.kittiwake-books.com
See detailed descriptions at www.davidberrywalks.co.uk

Walks on the **Clwydian Range** – 22 walks
More Walks on the **Clwydian Range** – 23 walks
Walks in the **Vale of Clwyd** – 22 walks
Walks around **Llangollen & the Dee Valley** – 25 walks
Walks around **Holywell & Halkyn Mountain** – 20 walks
Walks in the **Hidden Heart of North Wales** – 21 walks
Walks around the **Berwyn Mountains & the Ceiriog Valley** – 32 walks
Walks around **Betws-y-Coed & the Conwy Valley** – 24 walks
Walks in the **Heart of Snowdonia** – 36 walks
Walks on the **Llŷn Peninsula** – 30 walks
Walks around **Y Bala & Penllyn** – 20 walks
Walks around **Barmouth & the Mawddach Estuary** – 20 walks
Walks around **Anglesey (Ynys Môn)** – 40 walks
Walks around **Conwy & the Foothills of Northern Snowdonia**– 30 walks
Walks around **Ruabon Mountain, The Clywedog Valley & Hope Mountain** –
    28 walks
Walks around **Llandudno & along the coast to Prestatyn** – 30 walks
Walks around **Penmachno & Ysbyty Ifan** – 24 walks
Walks around **Chester & The Dee Estuary** – 26 walks
Walks around **Bangor & Caernarfon** – 22 walks
Best Coastal Walks in North Wales – 30 walks
Walks in **Hidden Conwy** – 25 walks
Best Walks in Northern Snowdonia – 30 walks

Long distance walks

The Conwy Valley Way – a 102 mile walk around the Conwy Valley
The Dee Way – 142 miles from Prestatyn or Hoylake through Chester and
Llangollen to the source
The Mawddach-Ardudwy Trail – a 94 mile walk connecting Barmouth,
Dolgellau, Harlech and Porthmadog

KITTIWAKE

Walks guides which detail superb routes
in most parts of Wales.

From Anglesey and Llandudno to the Brecon Beacons,
and from Machynlleth and Welshpool to Pembrokeshire and the Llŷn,
and including the borders, they offer a range
of carefully researched routes with something for all abilities.

Each guide has been compiled and written by a
dedicated author who really knows their particular area.

They are all presented in the **KITTIWAKE** clear
and easy-to-use style

For latest details of the expanding range, visit:

www.kittiwake-books.com

KITTIWAKE
3 Glantwymyn Village Workshops
Glantwymyn, Machynlleth
Montgomeryshire SY20 8LY